HENRY WINSTANLEY
AND THE
EDDYSTONE LIGHTHOUSE

HENRY WINSTANLEY

AND THE

EDDYSTONE LIGHTHOUSE

ADAM HART-DAVIS

and EMILY TROSCIANKO

SUTTON PUBLISHING

First published in 2002 by
Sutton Publishing Limited
Phoenix Mill · Thrupp · Stroud · Gloucestershire · GL5 2BU

Paperback edition first published in 2003

Copyright © Adam Hart-Davis and Emily Troscianko

All rights reserved. No part of this publication may be
reproduced, stored in a retrieval system, or transmitted, in any
form, or by any means, electronic, mechanical, photocopying,
recording or otherwise, without the prior permission of the
publisher and copyright holders.

Adam Hart-Davis and Emily Troscianko have asserted the moral
right to be identified as the authors of this work.

British Library Cataloguing in Publication Data
A catalogue record for this book is available from the British
Library

ISBN 0 7509 3379 8

Typeset in 14/17pt Perpetua.
Typesetting and origination by
Sutton Publishing Limited.
Printed and bound in England by
J.H. Haynes & Co. Ltd, Sparkford.

CONTENTS

LIST OF PLATES

(between pp. 96 and 97)

PREFACE

During the 1990s I presented on television a series of programmes called *Local Heroes*, in which I cycled around Britain (and occasionally other places) telling the stories of long-dead scientists, inventors and entrepreneurs – people who had left a mark on the world and were recognized as heroes, at least in their own home towns. We used to look for heroes for the series by telephoning local studies libraries and asking for potential candidates. A librarian in Plymouth suggested that I should read Fred Majdalaney's book *The Red Rocks of Eddystone*. When I did so I was captivated by the story of Henry Winstanley and his lighthouse, and I soon wanted to find out more and write my own book.

Finding out more proved a difficult task. Henry himself wrote little, and his contemporaries were not much better. I have visited what is supposed to be his birthplace, Winstanley House in Saffron Walden, and received much help and support from the library there. By what I consider a cunning piece of detective work I believe I have pinpointed the position of the house he built himself in Littlebury – the site of Winstanley's Wonders. In Audley End, the stately home where he worked for many years and made the acquaintance of King Charles II, I have recorded part of a radio programme about him, and also, rather incongruously, was filmed dressed as a monk in and around the walled garden. I have trodden the ground near Hyde Park Corner where he built his Waterworks. I have stood on the Barbican in Plymouth to tell the tale for radio of how he defied the advice of the fishermen and went out to Eddystone for that fatal last time. But above all I have been out to Eddystone: I have rowed between the ragged rocks, and even landed on the very rock where he built his lighthouse and later came to grief. Sitting on that rock, while the boat pulled away, was a moving and memorable experience.

This is the story of a remarkable man, his considerable achievements and his tragic end.

Adam Hart-Davis
January 2002

ACKNOWLEDGEMENTS

In our research for this book we have been helped by a great number of people, and would like to record our thanks to the following (with apologies to any we have inadvertently omitted): Bishopsgate Institute Library (Mr Webb); Bodleian Library, Oxford (John Johnson collection – Julie Anne Lambert); Dr Allan Chapman; Dr Michael Chrimes; City of Plymouth Museums & Art Gallery (Maureen Attril and others); City of Westminster Archives (Colin Recketts); Essex Record Office (Janet Smith); Guildhall Library (Jeremy Smith); Henley Library (Hilary Fisher); Tony Jago and his crew; Dr Peter Jones; Museum of London (Hazel Forsyth and Nicky Cross); Newmarket Library (Susan Thorpe); Portcullis Pursuivant of Arms; Public Record Office, Kew; Saffron Walden Library and Arts Centre (Martyn Everett); Saffron Walden Museum (Bruce Tice); Science Museum; Science Museum Library (Mrs P. Shah); Allen Simpson; The British Museum; Theatre

Acknowledgements

Museum (Melanie Trifona Christoudia); Trinity House Lighthouse Service (Breda Wall and Jane Wilson); Victoria & Albert Museum; West Devon Record Office (Rachel Broomfield); W.R.W. Winstanley. In addition our thanks go to those who have supplied pictures for this book.

Above all we thank Jaqueline Mitchell and her colleagues at Sutton, who provided masses of encouragement, and kept this book going long after others might have given up.

TIMELINE

Timeline

Timeline

He erected the first Eddystone light-house,
which he began in 1696 and finished four years
after. But, on the 26th November 1703, he was in
the light-house, superintending some repairs,
when there came on the most terrible tempest
which was ever known in England; and,
on the next morning, not a vestige of the building
was to be seen. It had been swept into the deep
from the foundation, not a stone, or beam,
or iron bar remaining on the rock.
Such was the melancholy fate of poor Winstanley!
– G.S.

Advertisement, 1709, in *Exhibitions of Mechanical and other Works of Ingenuity*, BL 1269 h.38, f. 105.

THE EDDYSTONE

The troubled Ocean *like a Caldron boils,*
And vomits up its long devoured Spoils . . .
Mountains of Water *in the* Air *do glide,*
Waves *on the back of* Waves *in Triumph ride . . .*

It is the land, not the sea, that makes a storm lethal to sailors. Out in the open sea, a good ship, well sailed, can get through most of what the skies might fling at it, but being blown on to the rocks leads always to disaster; as Daniel Defoe writes in his book, *The Storm*: 'The Fury of the Sea is the least thing our sailors fear: Keep them but from a *Lee Shore*, or touching upon a Sand, they'll venture all the rest.' Nevertheless, few sailors enjoy the fury of an Atlantic gale, and given the chance most would willingly take refuge in a safe haven – perhaps in one of the Channel ports. But the south Devon coast is as dangerous as any in the British Isles. Since records began, no fewer than 1,495 shipwrecks have been documented along its 90 miles, almost one wreck for every hundred yards of shore — and those are the ones we know about. Added to the usual dangers of a lee shore are those of rocks further out; barely sticking out of the water at high tide, they can be seen and avoided with difficulty, and can tear through a ship's hull with frightening ease.

As a ship runs from a growing gale in the Atlantic for shelter in the English Channel, the lights of a town suddenly flicker through the darkness and the spray to the north-east. Could it be Plymouth? Sighs of relief from the crew, since the headlands on either side of Plymouth Sound and the mouth of the Tamar river offer renowned and longed-for protection from the westerly winds. But 14 miles south-south-west of Plymouth lies a trap that has caught hundreds of sailors grown confident too early. Three ridges of rocky spikes spring up from the deep sea, one running approximately north–south, the other two splaying outwards from it. At low tide each ridge shows above the water for perhaps 300 yards, resembling

The Eddystone

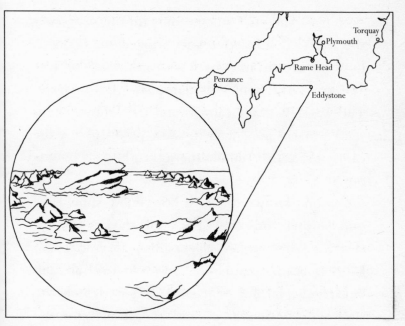

The viciously jagged and deadly Eddystone Reef, 14 miles south-south-west of Plymouth, 10 miles south of Rame Head. (*Jolyon Troscianko*)

a child's drawing of crocodile teeth, but at high tide only the two central rocks are visible; they just pierce the surface of a calmish sea, but are hidden by a heavy swell.

This cluster of rocks rises straight up from the depths, so there are rarely breakers to advertise its presence. And, as a steep mountain towering over the sea floor, it interferes with the water's normal flow and creates its own deadly maelstrom of tides and currents; hence its name, the Eddy-stone. The water is never calm round the Eddystone; as the Victorian poet Jean Ingelow puts it, '. . . the calmest seas that tumble there/Froth like a boiling pot'.

No one knows for sure how many ships have gone down on this 'rock of dark renown' (Ingelow). The square-riggers *Half Moon* in 1673, HMS *Coronation* and HMS *Harwich* in 1691 all sank before the fateful year of 1695, in which the sinking of *Snowdrop* and *Constant* spurred Winstanley to action. In the eighteenth century the sailing vessel *Marseilles* sank on 6 May 1746, and on 18 August 1756 the brig *Pelican*, en route from Spain, was lost with all hands. In August 1792 the brig *Grampus* from Whitehaven sank on her maiden voyage. Even in the nineteenth and twentieth centuries, with lighthouses to warn them off, at least forty ships are known to have met their end here, but records from before the nineteenth century are scant. They often tell us no more than that a ship set sail on a given date, never to be seen again. A wreck on an inhabited shore might provide identifiable washed-up remnants – or even survivors – and the information find its way back to the owners; but a ship that sank at Eddystone could easily do just that – sink, unnoticed, to the bottom. Wreckage rarely drifted the 14 miles into Plymouth – and how many can swim so far in a stormy sea?

The countless ships lost on the rock itself are, furthermore, only a fraction of what it has to answer for; in his biography of the great eighteenth-century engineer John Smeaton, who later built his own lighthouse on Eddystone, Samuel Smiles explains the additional toll:

> To avoid this terrible rock, the navigator was accustomed to give it as wide a berth as possible, and homeward-bound ships accordingly entered the Channel on a much more southerly parallel of latitude than they now do. In his solicitude to avoid the one danger, the sailor too often ran foul of another; and hence the numerous wrecks which formerly occurred

along the French coast, more particularly upon the dangerous rocks which surround the Islands of Jersey, Guernsey, and Alderney.

Eddystone was a perfectly placed peril. Plymouth has always been an important port. During the Hundred Years War against France, Plymouth provided 26 ships and 603 men for Edward III in the battle of Crécy in 1346 and the siege of Calais a few months later. In 1588, on the grassy clifftop above the Sound known as Plymouth Hoe, Francis Drake is supposed to have ignored the approaching Spanish Armada in favour of his game of bowls. In 1620 the Pilgrim Fathers set out from Plymouth in the *Mayflower* on a hazardous three-month crossing of the North Atlantic, and the captain noted the Eddystone in his log:

a wicked reef of twenty-three rust-red rocks lying nine and one half miles south of Rame Head on the Devon mainland, great ragged stones around which the sea constantly eddies, a great danger to all ships hereabouts, for they sit astride the entrance to this harbour and are exposed to the full force of the westerly winds and must always be dreaded by mariners. Leaving Plymouth, we managed to avoid this reef but ships making harbour must stand well to the south and this is difficult in stormy weather, for if any vessel makes too far to the south as likely as not she will be caught in the prevailing strong current and swept to her doom on those evil rocks.

Trade with the New World swelled year after year, but the city's status as a major port was compromised by the famous danger, which those wanting a share of the spoils had to avoid. On her travels in 1698 the diarist Celia Fiennes sketched the town as a picturesque port menaced by the seas:

Plymouth is 2 Parishes called the old town and the new, the houses built of this marble and the slatt at the top lookes like lead and glisters in the sun; there are noe great houses in the town; the streetes are good and clean, there is a great many tho' some are but narrow . . . up to the town there is a depth of water for shipps of the first rate to ride; its great sea and dangerous, by reason of the severall poynts of land between which the sea runs up a great way, and there are severall little islands alsoe, all which bears the severall tydes hard one against the other . . . The mouth of the river just at the town is a very good harbour for shipps; the Dock yards are about 2 mile from the town, by boate you goe to it the nearest way; its one of the best in England, a great many good shipps built there, and the great depth of water which comes up to it, tho' it runs up for 2 mile between the land, which also shelters the ships . . .

The end of the seventeenth century was a turbulent time for the British monarchy. In February 1685 the fun-loving Charles II died, and his brother became king, but James II was immensely unpopular, especially for trying to reinstate Roman Catholicism. When his wife Mary produced a son who was widely (though wrongly) believed to be someone else's baby, smuggled into her bedchamber in a warming pan, the country turned against him, and he fled for his life. In the Glorious Revolution of 1688, Prince William of Orange, married to James's daughter Mary, restored the Protestant supremacy. William brought his fleet of 400 ships into Plymouth, for a safe haven in what is now Devonport Dockyard.

Increasing American trade was making the port ever more prosperous. Prince William wanted this financial growth to continue unchecked by natural obstacles, and recognizing Eddystone's dangers he decreed that a lighthouse should be built on it as a warning to approaching ships. However, recognizing and decreeing were only the start of the solution.

In response to this royal incitement, the accomplishments (or lack of them) of one Walter Whitfield were destined to echo those of a pair of similarly ineffectual gentlemen, Sir John Coryton and Henry Brouncker. Thirty years earlier, in 1665, Coryton and Brouncker had made a petition to the Admiralty at Trinity House for leave to erect 'certain lighthouses' on the southern and south-western coasts of England, at that time entirely unlit. They suggested placing 'coal-fire lights' in a number of prime positions, including on the Scilly Isles, the Lizard, Portland Bill and the Eddystone. But Trinity House, the authority in charge of lighthouses then as now, while simultaneously acknowledging the necessity of a lighthouse, dismissed the Eddystone as a rock upon which any building work 'could hardly be accomplished'. Whether they were discouraged by this dampening response, or perhaps simply decided that they would rather avoid danger and stay rich, Coryton and Brouncker allowed their plans to sink out of sight, as the ships continued to do.

Whitfield's application to build a light on Eddystone, made in 1692, was likewise withdrawn when he realized how unattractive the terms would be. Trinity House decreed that the architect was to design and build the lighthouse at his own expense, and then recover the costs by collecting dues from ships sailing up the Channel which would benefit from its existence. But the rates stipulated were such that the outlay would not be recouped for decades: Trinity House considered that two pence per ton of ship would be quite enough, and, moreover, that 'the natives of his majesty's kingdoms' should be exempt from payment altogether. And on top of these discouraging terms was the high risk of failure. Eddystone was a protrusion of sloping slimy wave-dashed rock, hard enough to land upon, let alone build upon.

Then, in the last days of 1695, the enterprising shipowner Henry Winstanley was sitting having a quiet drink in a London pub when two bedraggled sailors staggered in and announced that one of his ships had sunk. On her way into Plymouth on Christmas Eve the *Constant* had gone down on the Eddystone Reef.

> Then stepped two mariners down the street,
> With looks of grief and fear:
> 'Now if Winstanley be your name,
> We bring you evil cheer.'

Earlier that year the *Snowdrop* had gone down with her entire crew of sixty; now another vessel and more men had been destroyed by the Eddystone, spurring Winstanley to make the week-long journey, on horseback along rutted tracks, through the wilds of Devonshire to investigate:

> 'I will take horse,' Winstanley said,
> 'And see this deadly rock.'

11

What he found was a challenge that he could not resist. Engraver, engineer and entrepreneur, Henry Winstanley had enjoyed the patronage of King Charles II. He had built himself a house of wonders in Essex, and a fabulous amusement centre in London. He had become a nationally famous showman and a shipowner, but he believed himself destined for greater things; his ambition was insatiable. The new king had said there should be a lighthouse on the reef, but no one was prepared to build it. Here, at last, was a chance for Winstanley to show his calibre to the world. His bravery fuelled by ignorance and inexperience, he declared his intention of achieving the unachievable and building a lighthouse on Eddystone. As Smeaton later put it:

It would appear to those then best acquainted with them, that the difficulties necessarily attending such an undertaking, were likely to prove insuperable: and perhaps in reality it may have been a peculiar advantage to every undertaker, and to the undertaking itself, that no one could, previous to the actual commencement of the work, be fully sensible of the difficulties which would inevitably attend it; and which he must surmount or fail of success.

Had Winstanley known anything at all, in practical terms, about lighthouses, about rocks or about storms at sea, he would surely never have tried to satisfy his craving for fame by dabbling in such dangerous difficulties.

AUDLEY END

Too large for a King, though it might do for a Lord Treasurer.

The seeds of Winstanley's rise to notoriety, sown by royal appreciation of his talents, sprouted within the elegance of Audley End, a manor house lying a mile west of Saffron Walden, spread beside the River Cam and the main London–Cambridge road (see plate section). Originally an abbey, it had been given by Henry VIII to Sir Thomas Audley on 27 March 1538 after the Dissolution of the Monasteries. In the early 1600s Thomas Howard, the 1st Earl of Suffolk, aspiring to create the most impressive private house in England, commissioned a wooden model from Italy at the very stylish price of £500, and began in 1603 a renovation process that took a dozen years. James I, who visited the house in 1610 and again in 1614, when it was still unfinished, remarked astutely that the house was too large for a king, though it might do for a Lord Treasurer.

Fifty years later the 3rd Earl could no longer afford to live in his vast sprawling mansion, and was on the lookout for a wealthy tenant. When the Great Plague swept through London in 1665 the charms of the countryside suddenly appeared more seductive, and Audley End seemed the perfect place for Charles II to hold court.

Charles had had a rough childhood, an unhappy mixture of illness and exile. Born in St James's Palace on 29 May 1630, the boy was somewhat weakly despite his wilful vivacity; he became very ill after breaking his arm at the age of nine, and when he caught measles in Reading he was left behind and was most disappointed to miss the king's march to London. When he was only twelve he and his younger brother James were almost captured at the Battle of Edgehill. He could hardly overlook his father's growing unpopularity with both Parliament and people: just before his sixteenth birthday, his life under threat and a price of £1,000 on his head, he obeyed his anxious father's orders and sailed away to safety.

Charles I was executed in 1649, and Charles II was proclaimed king in Edinburgh and Dublin, but in only one or two places in England. Eleven years passed before he was able to make a triumphant landing at Dover. 'Infinite the crowd of people and the horsemen, citizens, and noblemen of all sorts', writes Samuel Pepys in his diary. 'The shouting and the joy expressed by all is past imagination . . .'. After a splendid procession via Canterbury to London – 'So glorious was the show with gold and silver, that we were not able to look at it, our eyes at last being so much overcome' – Charles found both houses of Parliament waiting to greet him. Once officially king, Charles summoned his new Parliament and after leaving public curiosity to grow for a while – 'The talk of the town now is, who the King is like to have for his Queen' – at its first meeting took the opportunity to announce his engagement to Catherine of Braganza, the daughter of the King of Portugal.

This news, added to the recent overthrow of the Puritan influence, and the restoration of a tall and striking king, inspired much-needed confidence after the defeat of his diminutive father by Cromwell's armies, and the seven unsettled years of the Commonwealth. What better excuse for over-indulgence. Charles was exuberant and showy in mind and body. He liked to crown his swarthy 'fierce countenance' with a flowing dark periwig, a habit that quickly became a London trend; he liked flashy French fashions (except when war was declared against the French, when he had to resort to a pseudo-Persian style); he liked walking, dancing, tennis, hunting and going to the races; but he loved only women.

The royal wedding, in 1662, was celebrated at Winchester with suitable ostentation, but Charles unfortunately took an instant dislike to his bride, who had probably been chosen less for her personal attributes and more for her attractive dowry — £300,000 cash and the naval bases of Bombay and Tangier. The union allied the powers of England and Portugal, and brought England new territories and trading privileges, as well as two million Portuguese Crowns — but it gave Charles little sexual satisfaction. Not only did he keep his current mistress, Mrs Palmer, and make her Lady Castlemaine, but he arranged for her to become one of the ladies of the queen's bedchamber. Understandably indignant, Catherine dismissed most of her staff, but was in the end persuaded to retain the services of her low-born rival.

The diarist John Evelyn disapproved of all the king's affairs with characteristic prudishness, denouncing Lady Castlemaine with special bluntness as another 'Lady of Pleasure and the curse of our Nation'. However, Lady Castlemaine was far from being the only rival the queen had to contend with. When Charles went to Oxford in 1681, to fortify himself for the tedium of a parliamentary session with a day at the races, he stayed at Christ Church while the queen was banished to Merton, 100 yards from the back gate. His two mistresses, the Duchess of Portsmouth and Nell Gwyn, lodged in the town – quite near enough . . .

Catherine's Catholic faith and inability to produce an heir created tension between Charles and his ministers, but although he may not have loved her much he did not want to abandon her or to see her killed. When she was accused of trying to poison him, and charged with high treason, he prevented the trial from taking place, whether or not the charges were just. A second refusal to let his ministers ruin his marriage came in his rejection of their attempts to arrange a divorce on the grounds of Catherine's infertility.

Nevertheless, Charles reserved his real tenderness for his mistresses. 'He hath not missed one night since she was sick, of supping with my Lady Castlemaine,' says Pepys, on the good authority of the wife of the man who prepared their illicit suppers. As for the short, sweet actress Nell Gwyn, Pepys found her such a 'mighty pretty soul' that after seeing her in one performance at the theatre neither he nor his wife could resist kissing her. In about 1669 she had recited a monologue wearing a hat the size of a large coach-wheel, which so effectively set off the delicacy of her figure that the king was induced to invite her to supper, and thence to bed. She remained his mistress, on and off, for many years, and bore him two sons. (Evelyn

Some of the King's Mistresses

Lady Castlemaine

Originally Mrs Palmer, Charles made her Lady Castlemaine after his marriage, and appointed her a lady of the queen's bedchamber. She cost him more than his affections, though: in one month he spent about £30,000 paying off her debts. She thought nothing of winning £15,000 in a night at the card-table – and losing twice as much the night after, regularly staking over a thousand pounds on the turn of a card or the roll of a die.

The Duchess of Portsmouth

The Catholic Louise de Kéroualle or Quérouaille came from Brittany, and was suspected by many – with some reason – of being a spy sent by Louis XIV; as a result she was most unpopular with the British public. She had a son by Charles in 1672, and persuaded him to sign with Louis a secret treaty giving more freedom to Catholics. She was known by her new compatriots as Mrs Carwell before Charles made her a duchess.

Nell Gwyn

As a child, Eleanor Gwyn sold oranges outside Drury Lane Theatre in London. She became an actress of charm and renown, who appeared in many London plays by John Dryden and others, several of whom wrote parts specially for her. Samuel Pepys was one of hundreds struck by her comeliness; he called her 'pretty, witty Nell'.

Nell was a rival to the Catholic Duchess of Portsmouth for the king's love, and when she was mobbed in Oxford, she leaned out of her carriage window and appealed to the crowd: 'Pray, good people, be civil; I am the *Protestant* whore.' In the words of a contemporary rhymester: 'She's now the darling strumpet of the crowd/forgets her state, and talks to them aloud . . .'

Rumours that Charles also had an underground passage dug between Newmarket Palace and what is now Gwynn House in Palace Street, so that he could pursue his pleasures more discreetly, are appealing but unlikely, since he rarely bothered to hide his liaisons.

naturally thought Charles far too intimate with this 'impudent Comedian'.) Loved dearly by the king, she filled his last thoughts; when he died, on 6 February 1685, he was attended certainly by the Duchess of Portsmouth, and possibly by the queen – but his final words were 'Let not poor Nelly starve!'

For the king, then, Audley End had two great added advantages in addition to its proximity to London and its carefully cultivated impressiveness. It was only 15 miles from the races at Newmarket and only 3 miles from Newport, where he was able to find a house for Nell Gwyn. John Evelyn testifies to Audley End's undeniable material attractions:

From Cambridge, on August 31, 1654, we went to Audley End, and spent some time in seeing that goodly palace . . . It is a mixt fabrick, twixt antiq and modern . . . and it is one of the stateliest palaces of the kingdom. It consists of two courts, the first very large, winged with cloisteres. The front hath a double entrance. The hall is faire, but somewhat too small for so august a pile. The kitchen is very large, as are the cellars, arched with stone, very neate and well disposed . . . The gallery is the most cheerful, and I

Audley End

The milestone at Audley End. (*Adam Hart-Davis*)

think one of the best in England; a faire dining-room, and the rest of the lodgings answerable, with a pretty chapel. The gardens are not in order, tho' well enclosed. It also has a bowling alley, and a nobly-well walled, wooded, and watered park. The river glides before the palace, to which is an avenue of lime trees . . . For the rest, it is a perfectly uniform structure, and shews without like a diadem, by the decorations of the cupolas and other ornaments on the pavilions.

Five years later Samuel Pepys was shown round by the housekeeper. 'The stateliness of the ceilings, chimney-pieces, and form of the whole was exceedingly worth seeing,' he reported. 'He took us into the cellar, where we drank, most admirable drink, a health to the King. Here I played on my fflageolette, there being an excellent echo . . .'. A couple of years later, visiting with his wife, the sharpness of his observations was again somewhat blunted, his convolutions lengthened, by too much lavish hospitality:

> Took coach to Audley End, and did go all over the house and garden, and mighty merry we were. The house indeed, do appear very fine . . . and above all things the cellars, where we went down and drank of much good liquors. And indeed the cellars are fine, and here my wife and I did sing to my great content. And then to the garden, and there did eat many grapes, and took some with us; and so away thence well satisfied . . .

With so many attractive features to lure him there, Charles visited Audley End frequently. According to the *London Gazette*, 'In the autumn of 1668, Charles II met the Queen and the ladies of her Court at Audley End, having been diverting himself for some time at Newmarket, and in visiting several forts and towns on the sea coast.' The king grew pleasantly accustomed to such jaunts, and finally, in May 1669, bought the house for the sum of £50,000, of which £20,000 was to remain on mortgage.

The king now had the country house he had been looking for, and the Earl of Suffolk, while retaining possession of the whole estate apart from 283 acres of parkland, was now able to pay off his considerable debts with the proceeds. The following year the Court was established at this 'New Palace', flooding the countryside with aristocrats. The king's handsome nephew William, Prince of Orange, stayed the night after receiving an honorary degree at Cambridge. A letter of 13 October 1670 to Sir Robert Paston from Nathaniel Henshaw, an Irish physician and Fellow of the Royal

Society, recounts the ladies' attempted espousal of quaint country habits:

> Last week, there being a Faire neare Audley End, the Queen, the Dutchess of Richmond, and the Dutchess of Buckingham, had a frolick to deguise themselves like country lasses, in red petticotes, wastcotes, &c. and so goe see the Faire . . . They had all so overdone it in their deguise, and look'd so much more like Antiques (i.e. actors) than country volk, that as soone as they came to the Faire the people began to goe after them. But the Queen going to a booth to buy a paire of yellow stockins for her swete hart . . . they were soon, by their gebrish, found to be strangers, which drew a bigger flock about them. One amongst them had seen the Queen at dinner, knew her, and was proud of her knowledge: this soon brought all the Faire into a crowd to stare at the Queen. Being thus discovered, they, as soon as they could, got to their horses . . . Thus, by ill conduct, was a merrie frolick turned into a pennance.

The king had other, and less abortive, 'merrie frolicks' to pursue. He often decamped to Newmarket for days at a time, living in the only part of the palace there that had remained unravaged by Cromwell. The exotic Hortense, Duchess of Mazarin, set up her notorious gambling den in Newmarket, so beguiling Charles with the size of the stakes and her feminine wiles that he jettisoned the Duchess of Portsmouth, who grew pale and thin. Nell Gwyn was delighted, and went into ostentatious mourning for the social death of her Catholic rival.

For many happy months the king organized his daily schedule not around state duties but around the priorities of a morning at the Duchess of Cleveland's, before she rose, an afternoon at a cockfight or the races, and an evening at the theatre. In the duchess's bed he first met Frances Teresa Stuart, later the Duchess of Richmond. Frances's beauty was undisputed; Pepys, that great connoisseur of the female form, adds his voice to the general resounding praise of her:

Mrs. Stewart in this dress, with her hat cocked and a red plume, with her sweet eye, little Roman nose, and excellent taille, is now the greatest beauty I ever saw, I think, in my life; and, if ever woman can, do exceed my Lady Castlemaine, at least in this dress: nor do I wonder if the King changes, which I verily believe is the reason of his coldness to my Lady Castlemaine.

Despite the oft-quoted observation of the Earl of Rochester that the king 'never said a foolish thing, nor ever did a wise one', Charles proved himself a more practical and hard-headed ruler than his chaotic love-life would suggest. He was perhaps more cynical than artless; so much so that, as Lord Halifax remarked, his ministers learned to watch his face as he talked, judging it 'of more importance to see than to hear what he said'. Between his adventures Charles returned to Audley End to hold court in more sumptuous surroundings than the crumbling palace at Newmarket could afford. Charles was an infallible judge of character and it was at his country mansion that he became impressed by an enterprising young man who worked on the estate, and soon promoted him to Clerk of Works. This young unknown was the ingenious Henry Winstanley.

An Ingenious Engraver

Every artist writes his own autobiography.

Henry Winstanley was only twenty-five when he was made Clerk of Works in the king's service at Audley End and Newmarket, having been employed at Audley End as a porter for some five years. He was already beginning to show signs of the innovative showmanship and social ambition that would eventually prove his downfall. To begin with they simply made him impatient to escape his humble origins.

We know little of Winstanley's early life. He was born into a well-known local family in Saffron Walden in 1644, supposedly in Winstanley House, on the corner of the Cockpit, 20 yards from the market place. His father, also called Henry, enjoyed a varied career as mercer, Master of the Alms-houses, steward at Audley End and, for the five years before his death in 1680, as churchwarden of

Saffron Walden. Our Henry had an elder sister Susannah, who married Benjamin Newbolt in 1692, and two younger brothers, Robert (born 1646) and Charles. Charles had two sons, Henry and William; our Henry himself married a local girl, Jane Taylor, but they had no children, although according to one source they had a son: Hamlet Winstanley (1695-1756), artist, portrait painter and engraver, is generally believed to have been Henry's nephew, but Horace Walpole's extracts from the manuscripts of George Vertue state that Henry was his father.

Perhaps Henry's uncle William Winstanley was an influence in his youth. 'A true lover of ingenuity' was what he liked modestly to call himself; others called him Will. Having started his career as a barber, he made himself famous (some would say infamous) by abandoning the razor for the pen. Critics claimed that he never really gave up the scissors, for although he was a would-be 'fantastical writer' he unashamedly plagiarized other authors.

With his own work, unfortunately, he was not as good at shaping and trimming, and he poured forth large quantities of indiscriminate quality. He churned out reams of poetry and at least a dozen books, including *Lives of the Most Famous English Poets* and *England's worthies — select lives of the most eminent persons of the English nation, from Constantine the Great, down to these times*. The feeble ending to the chapter on Chaucer reads: 'Geoffrey Chaucer, no friend to the covetous and leacherous Clergy-men of those times, was fined two shillings for beating of a Franciscan Frier in Fleet-street: a considerable sum, since Money was so scarce in those days.' More popular than his polemics were his forays into pseudo-science. In about 1661 he started *Poor Robin's Almanack*, an annual compilation of astrological predictions, calendar information, jokes and helpful lifestyle hints, which flourished for more than a century.

So Henry grew up in a noteworthy family in a thriving market town. He probably got his first job as porter at Audley End because his father was steward there, and allowed him to run informal errands. When he acquired an official post he must have been busy carrying messages and doing minor chores all over the vast house and estate. We know

Poor Robin, 1742.

AN
ALMANACK

After the Old and New Fashion:

Wherein

The Reader may see (if he be not blind) many remarkable Things, worthy of Observation.

Containing a two-fold Calendar;

Viz. The *Julian,* or *English,* and the Roundheads, or Fanaticks ; with their several Saints Days, and Observations upon each Month.

Being the second after BISSEXTILE, or Leap-Year.

Written by POOR ROBIN *Knight of the Burnt-Island, a Well-Wisher to the Mathematicks.*

While others tell you strange surprising Things,
Of Wars in foreign Countries, Death of Kings ;
Such Things as these are least of all our Cares,
Because we meddle not with State Affairs :
Our Business is to tell when't's Holiday,
When People ought to work, and when to play.
The Truth of our Predictions will appear,
If you have Patience but another Year.

LONDON, Printed for the Company of *Stationers,* 1742.

A sample of William Winstanley's almanac. It obviously flourished for many years.

(*Saffron Walden Library*)

from his later achievements that he had a mechanical bent, and there must have been plenty of opportunities to display his skill; fixing squeaky doors and guttering lamps and rattling windows would have been second nature to the resourceful young Mr Winstanley. No doubt he would have been able to earn generous tips from all the varied and important visitors. He was able and energetic, and his enterprising nature won him favour first with the Earl of Suffolk and then with the king when he appeared with his court in tow – which is why Henry was promoted to Clerk of Works in 1669.

As well as enjoying the responsibility of his new post, which inched him closer to the rich and powerful, Winstanley began to make inroads into engineering. His ingenuity brought him to the king's attention and he was advised to go abroad; he travelled in France, Germany and Italy. In Italy especially, many small mechanical devices and toys caught his eye, and he started contriving some himself, continuing this when he came home. His favourite items were illuminated fountains for dining tables.

Detail from the parish records showing the payment to Henry Winstanley for painting and contriving the dial and motion in the church. (*Saffron Walden Library*)

In 1679 he constructed an intricate mechanism for the Saffron Walden church clock. A set of clockwork-driven hammers played chimes on eight bells, embellished by rising and setting spheres to represent the sun and moon. His father, then the churchwarden, recorded the transaction in the accounts. At £8, the clock was an extravagant investment for a parish church, and its price serves as the first concrete testimony to Winstanley's creative flair.

Meanwhile Henry had conquered an entirely different territory through persistence if not panache. He somehow learned, probably by teaching himself, copper line engraving. The European roots of copper engraving go back to the goldsmiths of fifteenth-century Florence, who used ornamental engravings filled with black enamel to enliven gold frames and plates. Their biggest problem was that the design was invisible before the enamel was added; to resolve this they would make a sulphur cast of the half-finished engraving in a clay mould, and fill the carved lines filled with lamp-black (soot from a lamp) so that they stood out. Then someone had the bright idea of turning the process on its head, and using dampened paper to make an impression from these black lines. After filling the lines in the metal with ink and wiping any spills from the smooth surface, they rolled dampened paper on to the plate with enough pressure to force the paper into the channels, where it soaked up the lines of ink. Now, instead of having a single piece of engraved metal, the engraver could run off many copies of his work on paper.

By Winstanley's time, engraving had been used as a method of reproduction in its own right for about a century. It was efficient and easy, at least technically, and needed only a modest outlay: a sheet of metal, some sort of roller and the chiselling tool (the burin), which is carefully pushed, rather than pulled, across the surface of the metal. The technique takes some getting used to, and Henry

Engravings and Woodcuts

Line Engraving

The lines of the image are scratched into the metal (or sometimes wooden) plate using a sharp tool, and then soft ink is applied to the whole surface, making sure that it fills all the lines. Then all the ink on the flat unscratched surface is wiped off, and soft, dampened paper laid down and pressed on to the surface with rollers, so that it is pushed into all the lines, and soaks up the ink to collect the image. This is called intaglio printing.

Etching

The metal surface is first coated with an inert material such as wax, then the lines of the image are scratched through the wax with a sharp tool like a needle. The metal plate is then dipped in a bath of acid. This does not affect the wax, but where the wax has been scratched away the acid eats into the metal surface. Then the acid is washed away, the wax removed and the plate is treated with ink exactly as in line engraving.

Mezzotint

The metal surface is roughened all over with a 'rocker', and then parts of it are smoothed with scrapers to produce the image. Ink is then applied and the paper is pressed on. The pure rough areas produce rich deep black on the paper, while the areas scraped clear come up white, and a great range of tones can be produced. There are no hard lines, only subtle shading achieved by the varying roughness of the surface of the metal.

Woodcut

The artist draws the image on a piece of wood, traditionally cherry or pear wood, and then carefully cuts away the wood all round the lines, to leave the image standing out in relief. The whole surface is then inked with a roller, absorbent paper is laid on top and pressed down with a spoon or a roller, and then carefully peeled of from one corner to give the final image. The woodcut was the earliest form of image printing, but was eclipsed by line engraving, since the latter gave results at once more precise and more powerful.

must have spent hours crouched over his copper plates, carefully gouging away the metal. He would probably have started by practising straight lines, progressing to curves, then crossing them to form squares, lozenges and triangles. Later perhaps he found some prints to copy.

The difference between Winstanley and the majority of engravers at the time is that he preferred to concoct his own designs, rather than copy the paintings of others. This was a far more risky enterprise: there was a ready trade in engravings of famous paintings – indeed, it was by such engravings that many works of art became well known – while producing original prints of buildings, famous people, comic scenes or other designs meant making a market of one's own.

Winstanley repeatedly, cannily and duplicitously asserted that his goal was not primarily to make money; rather he was an artist, exploring a new art form. Copying someone else's work would not have sat easily with his arrogant ambition. In the early days he had a penchant for elaborate domestic scenes, such as one featuring a long-haired and beribboned gentleman and a seductively clad and ringletted lady. They sit eating al fresco on a veranda framed by curtains and columns, with a good-looking page-boy and a well-stocked wine-cooler in the background. Servants and balconies were nothing new, but such images of upper-class idylls illustrate Winstanley's fascination with wealth and gentility.

Then he turned his attention from the habits of the rich to their habitats. The restoration of Audley End was typical of a trend for country house building among the affluent that lasted throughout the seventeenth century, and was particularly prevalent in the years after the Restoration, peaking during the 1690s. Winstanley was not alone in channelling off some of this conspicuous wealth by recording the new architectural creations and selling the pictures of the houses back to their owners. On a much grander scale, the artists Johannes Kip and Leonard Knyff produced their *Britannia Illustrata*, containing eighty copperplate engravings of homes and gardens. Winstanley lacked both the reputation and the experience of such artists, but still managed to find patrons to commission engravings of their own stately homes. He engraved the manor house at Wimbledon, for instance, and dedicated his work to its noble and opulent owner Thomas, Earl of Danby. He used his views of Audley End as samples of his skill, and found, no doubt, that it was not without commercial advantage to know the king.

His engravings do not display phenomenal artistic ability, though perhaps more than does his uncle's poetry. Henry's clouds and landscapes are stylized rather than realistic as he presumably intended – the trees especially look more like those on modern maps than the real thing – and in close-up the eyes of his people are unconvincing. His views, especially of Audley End (see plate section), are valuable rather as a historical and architectural record, without which no one would really know now what the place looked like. His masterpiece was a set of twenty-four views of the house, each 2, 3 or even 4 feet wide, and all crammed with intricate detail of brickwork and pinnacles, turrets and tiles. He had them bound into a huge book, which he presented to his original employer with a letter of delicious sycophantic meandering:

To the right honourable James Earle of Suffolk
May it please your Lordship.

The Object of these my Labours, being a Fabrick of your noble Grandfather, I hope my endeavour to express the Magnificence of so great a Building (which continues to show in some considerable measure the Greatness of the Mind of so honourable an Ancestor) will not be displeasing to your Lordship; although it might be the subject of a learned Pen to describe the Architecture, Symmetry, and Situation of it.

I have performed the best of my Endeavours in delineating of the same, according to the Rules of Perspective: & having seen the most renowned Palaces of France, Germany, and Italy, especially from whence Architecture is brought over; & those making so great noise, as to encourage many to make Journeys to observe them, & this lying obscure and not took notice of, I thought it Injustice to the Founder, that he had left such a Monument to Posterity, had not the same Advantage, as to have his great works exposed to the View of the World.

Henry Winstanley

I most humbly beg Leave of your Lordship to say, you had a true value for it, when you was pleased to prefer it to so great a Master, as now it hath: & by that meanes it being not unworthily made a Royall Palace, I think it ought to be esteemed not inferior to any in this Kingdom, but equall to any in Europe.

I do not undertake to make an accurate Discourse of the many Advantages of this admirable Building; but my Care has been to take true Views of all, without striving to add any Fancy to that which is so perfect by itself: & if in these my Draughts I have given your Lordship any Satisfaction, I shall rejoice in it, & shall think myself most happy if in any Thing I can more express myself.

My Lord, your Lordship's most humble and most obedient servant

Hen: Winstanley

Two other copies of the work were dedicated respectively to Christopher Wren (who was for a time engaged at Audley End, and was no doubt interested in the building) and to James II, after he became king in 1685.

This letter is, alas, only a copy of the original, reported by Dr Erwin of Cambridge a hundred years later, but assuming it is an accurate copy Winstanley's consistent spelling makes a notable exception; most seventeenth-century writers were thoroughly capricious. One intriguing feature is the spelling of his name, which lacks this constancy; like his father and uncle, in this letter he spells Winstanley with an 'e', as is found on his poll tax receipt of 1692 and on most of his engravings. Yet on an engraving of 1699 he spells his name Winstanly, without an 'e'. Did he really not care? It seems unlikely.

The text of the dedication demonstrates that combination of obsequiousness and enthusiasm tempered with cunning that he and others commonly used to promote their talents. Winstanley's engraving of his own house at Littlebury showed in its first edition just the building with a hint of trees behind it, but later carried a giant advertisement in the sky: 'The undertaker of this great work can not be thought to design extraordinary profitt to himselfe considering ye charge of Copper Plates, and expenses of journeys especially to places farr remote to take designes &c . . .'.

With great self-sacrifice, he claimed, he had taken on the task of creating a volume of engravings to flaunt the attractions of English stately homes, which he considered just as grand as their continental counterparts. His book would allow armchair travellers to appreciate these architectural treasures without the hassle of actually going to visit them. The second part of the advertisement explains the proposed procedure:

> All Noble men and Gentlemen that please to have their Mansion Houses design'd on Copper Plates to be printed for composeing a volume of ye Prospects of ye Principall Houses of England. May have them done by Mr. Hen. Winstanley by way of Subscription, yt is to say, subscribing to pay five Pounds at ye delivering of a fair Coppy of their respective houses . . .

He also offered to supply for any house a painting in oils for a reasonable, though unspecified, fee; to supply extra prints from the volume of engravings at a bargain rate, and to deliver them free of charge. Who could resist such persuasive marketing? Could anyone who was anyone afford to be left out of such a volume? The fact that it was never completed may perhaps show that his opinion of his artistic skill was not shared by the great and the rich – or perhaps we should take it as evidence that his mind had flitted to higher things, such as his pretty packs of playing cards (see plate section).

People with money and time to spare in the withdrawing room after dinner were always looking for diversions and amusements. Playing card games was a slightly risqué pastime which appealed to ladies as well as gentlemen. By producing a set of educational cards, Winstanley was making them more acceptable to the puritanically minded – and jumping on to a money-making bandwagon.

During the late seventeenth century a fashion developed for playing cards that were 'educational'. They were ordinary cards suitable for playing games, but they also carried edifying information about law, theology, heraldry, mathematics, spelling, Latin grammar and especially geography. The theory was that the young people playing card games would be learning as they played. Winstanley's playing cards had a geographical theme, each featuring pictures of and comments about the countries and peoples of the world. There are the same fifty-two cards and four suits as are used today. The aces stand for continents – hearts for Europe, spades for Africa, diamonds for Asia, clubs for America. With predictable ethnocentricity, the text on the Europe card glows with the greatest pride:

> Europe is the least of the four parts of the world and yet is not much inferior to any at this present for containing many nations most polished and ingenious where arts and sciences flourish and are cherished, trading abounding and conversation without danger. She may boast her richness, fruitfulness, and stately towns and palaces, but above all in that the Christian religion is wholly professed in her bounds whereas the rest of the world is for the most part ignorant of a true deity . . .

Each of the other cards represents a nation and a city; for example, the three of hearts shows the 'Moscouites' in Moscow, the five of diamonds the

'Chilians' at St Iago and the four of hearts the 'Holanders' in Amsterdam. Each card has a picture of the people in their 'national dress' and a selection of buildings to give an impression of the place. Conventionally the most important information was put on the hearts, which meant that, since the aces were used as general categories, the most important card was usually the king of hearts. Winstanley's king of hearts shows Charles II and Catherine of Braganza with, in the background, the Thames, the old London Bridge and the monument designed by Christopher Wren and recently erected there to commemorate the Great Fire of London of 1666.

The accuracy of this card, and of those of the European cities he had visited or at least heard first-hand accounts of, would not have posed many problems for Winstanley, especially since his title sheet does acknowledge help: 'all which is most Humbly Presented and Dedicated to the Hon'ble James Herbert Esq. Not for his Improvement, But that it was part of his Studys and from Whom I must own I have received most of my Instructions in the Composing of these Cards . . .'. Nevertheless it seems likely that the details of 'national dress' and principal architecture for Greenland, China, Peru and Poland were largely made up – the fruits rather of the engraver's rich imagination than of careful reporting by a well-travelled observer.

The potential market for such playing cards was extensive – at least sixty-five different educational sets of playing cards were produced between 1675 and 1720 – which may have been one reason for Winstanley branching out in this direction. He produced his cards around 1675, but since no advertisements for them have been found it seems likely that he sold them only at his house of wonders and later at his waterworks. In any case he probably made a lot of money out of them. But fortune without fame was not enough; Winstanley wanted to be remembered by the whole world, for ever. In the end he came close to achieving his ambition – at least, his entry in the *Dictionary of National Biography* is longer than that of his master, James, Earl of Suffolk. And he climbed the next few rungs of the social ladder by becoming a builder.

FOUR

WINSTANLEY'S WONDERS

*The fam'd house of the . . . ingenious Mr Winstanly
. . . is on the Coach-road to Cambridge . . . and is
shewn for 12d each and to Livery men 6d. This is
known by a Lanthorn on the top of it.*

*I saw those ingenious Water-works invented by
Mr Winstanley wherein were some things very
surprising and extraordinary.*

In his thirties Henry Winstanley had married Jane
Taylor, but sadly all we know is that they had no
children. We have no information about whether
they were a devoted couple, nor whether she
traipsed around the country with him and assisted
in his later endeavours. Maybe he carried his new
bride tenderly over the threshold of the house he
had built, dreaming of marital bliss. Maybe he saw
his house as nothing more than a handy base, close
to the manor. Either way, Winstanley moved soon
after his marriage to Littlebury, only a mile or so
north of Audley End. With a current population of

around 800, Littlebury is still only a village, but it seems to have been a lively place in the seventeenth century. Barley was frequently being stolen from the tithe heaps; a warrant was issued to constables to search the houses of suspected poachers; and the community lived in dread of a juvenile pyromaniac called Alice.

This was the place in which Winstanley chose to build himself a spectacular house. Alas, it no longer exists; apparently it was demolished and the stones used for another building. Local legend, backed up by engraved plans of the property of Gilbert Marshall Esq. now in the Essex Record Office, suggests that the house stood in what is now an open field across the little road just to the south of the church. Furthermore, the map of Essex drawn a century later in the 1770s shows a house on this very site, opposite the church. Today such a house would merely be by the roadside, but comparison of old and modern maps shows that the roads around Littlebury have moved, most notably after the building of the iron bridge over the Cam in 1858, which allowed traffic to bypass the village. In the late seventeenth century anyone riding north from Audley End – or indeed heading from London towards Cambridge or Newmarket – would have rounded a sharp corner to be confronted with all the glory of Winstanley's construction, facing the main road and impossible to ignore.

The building itself was also conspicuous (see plate section); it had a windmill in the garden, a clock on the gable and on the roof an enormous lantern to attract visitors like fireflies. Instead of a normal garden gate there was a turnstile, for this was less a home than a seventeenth-century amusement arcade; visitors were paying customers rather than guests. Members of the public were welcome to pay a shilling each to be admitted and shown round the fantastical world of what its owner called Winstanley's Wonders.

It was a veritable House of Fun. There were distorting mirrors to transform visitors from wispy spirits to creatures as solid as cows. There was an old slipper lying on the floor just waiting to be kicked – and to unleash a ghost from the floorboards. There were trick chairs – one, according to a Mr Richard Lawson of Urmston, was a 'particularly comfortable-looking chair, which, when sat upon, instantly closed its arms around the occupant, making him a firm prisoner', and another scooted speedily backwards on a rail, through the French windows, to suspend the sitter above the stream in the back garden. If the unwary visitor sat in an arbour by the side of the stream, he was set afloat in the middle of it. This stream was artificial; water was pumped from the river by the windmill, which may also have powered some of the mechanisms, such as the 'clockwork organ' from which music emanated as if by magic.

People were hungry for this sort of fun; the diarist Celia Fiennes writes disappointedly of the 'abundance of fine Curiosityes all performed by clockwork and such like which appears very strange to the beholder but the master was not at home so I saw no more than the Chaire they set in when they are carryd about . . .'.

Mr and Mrs Usticke from Land's End made a tour of England on horseback – both on the back of the same horse, with their cousin on another for company – and ventured into the wilds of Essex especially to see the well-known Wonders. William Usticke's diary entry is enthusiastic on his cousin's behalf, though looking on was probably the more sensible option:

> One chair as my cousin Tresillian sat in it descended perpendicularly about ten feet in a dark and dismal place. Another as he sat in it ran ye length of a small orchard and over a moat, jumped in a tree, then descended and in a very little time stopped. A seat in ye garden was changed into several shapes . . . We gave each a shilling to see ye house.

One note of disapprovingly adult criticism is sounded by Mr Horace Walpole: 'These childish contrivances I suppose he learned in Italy where they do not let their religion monopolise all kinds of legerdemain.' But such vestiges of puritanism were rare; in general people were glad to take their cue from their fun-loving king and revel in the new diversions of the Restoration.

Charles II was a regular at the Wonder-House, and no doubt used to take tea with Henry and his wife. He genuinely admired the ingenuity of the place – he had given his blessing to the Royal Society and was all in favour of increasing the spread of science and technology – and used it as a good excuse to get away from Audley End in order to visit Nell Gwyn. He could hardly have dropped in for tea en route to her bedside, since Littlebury lay in the wrong direction, but the Wonders must have provided a useful smokescreen.

Basking in royal patronage, Henry swelled with pride. And to make his rise into the upper echelons of society quite clear to lesser mortals, he began to call himself 'Gent'. Technically, the term 'Gentleman' came into use in the fifteenth century to signify a condition between baron (or knight) and yeoman, but from the sixteenth century it was used more loosely to describe a way of life, a gentleman being someone who did not work with his hands. 'Gentleman' was also used to describe a man of good birth who was entitled to bear arms but was not a nobleman; often this meant the younger sons of nobility. Henry did work with his hands, and was not of noble birth – his father was an honest but title-less churchwarden. Furthermore, research by Portcullis Pursuivant of Arms reveals that although there were Winstanleys in Lancashire and Lincolnshire whose coats of arms were recorded by visitations in the 1660s, these did not include the Essex family, nor was there any mention of a Henry.

So Henry's usage of the term Gent was quite unjustified, but no doubt he felt he had earned it, and he began to use it on official documents. On 14 October 1692 the receipt for his poll tax read, 'These are to certify to all who it may concerne that Henry Winstanley Gentl as residing and dwelling within the parish of Littlebury is rated and assessed for his Title and Poll the sum of one and twenty shillings to the second quarterly payment of the said Poll Tax. All of which he hath paid . . .'.

The lesson Winstanley learned from his Wonders was that building could bring both money and intoxicating fame; now addicted, he reckoned that the easiest way for him to feed his habit was to keep on building. To the church that had already bought his clock he now added an equally unusual spire, which survived until 1831, when it was taken down. It was made conventionally, of wood covered with lead, but the spire had a vast lantern hanging a hundred feet or so above the ground, as if to guide believers away from the jagged rocks of sin. Perhaps Winstanley already had lighthouses on the brain.

Despite such successes, Littlebury and even Saffron Walden hardly counted as the centres of civilization; London was the place for him to really make his mark. So Winstanley set off for the metropolis, and in the early 1690s he completed his grandest project so far, a fabulous water theatre, or 'Waterworks'. Even twenty years later, on 23 April 1713, the *Guardian* was proud to announce 'The famous Water Theatre of the late ingenious Mr Winstanley . . . is at the lower end of Piccadilly, and is known by the windmill on top of it.' At that time Piccadilly petered out close to St James's Church, near where the Ritz Hotel now stands. After that it became the road to Exeter, running between St James's Park and open fields to the cross-roads that is now Hyde Park Corner. At this cross-roads stood a celebrated tavern, the Pillars of Hercules, where Squire Western stayed when he came to visit London in Henry Fielding's novel *Tom Jones*. Somewhere along the string of other pubs woven in among the cottages that lined the road here – the Golden Lion, the Red Lion, the Horse-Shoe, the Running Horse, the Swan, and the Barley Mow – was Winstanley's own establishment for liquid entertainment.

Winstanley's curiosity had precursors in various other central London attractions, including a floating restaurant called the Folly, moored opposite Somerset House, and even more bizarrely, according to an advertisement in the *London Gazette*, 'an entire Egyptian Mummy with all the hieroglyphics and skutcheons on it . . . It is the body of a Princely young lady . . . preserved in and with her coffin for 2,500 years without putrefecation . . . [It] may be seen by any person of quality at Mr. Savage's at the Head and Combe in the Strand.'

Winstanley's attraction was more conspicuously elaborate than these. The theatre itself was small and wooden, the focus of attention a great barrel in which the magic was worked. Into it poured, apparently by a single inlet, all sorts of liquids, from water to wine and milk. Out of it gushed fountains and sprays of water – which could even come from glass candelabra in which candles were burning. However, the central feature was that from a single tap poured either wine, beer, coffee or anything else the patrons might fancy. Never one to miss out on an opportunity for tactical flattery, Winstanley also erected a series of pulleys by which a coffee tray, hung from the ceiling and laden with cups, could be drawn to and fro and be presented to the most distinguished members of the audience.

The show was a heady cocktail of hydraulic trickery and pyrotechnics – all accompanied by the imposing strains of an organ, probably a clockwork one such as that he had perfected at the Wonder-House – and was a huge success. It was a place to see and be seen, to be amused and impressed. John Evelyn wrote about it on 20 June 1696: 'I saw those ingenious Water-works invented by Mr

Winstanley wherein were some things very surprising and extraordinary.'

The traveller and writer Zacharis Conrad von Uffenbach visited in 1710, and wrote:

> It is immediately behind St James Park and is an ordinary theatre, in which all kinds of water effects are represented. They all depend on the vat that stands in the middle, but the main mechanism could not be seen . . . Above on the ceiling there were pulleys, to which a coffee-tray was fastened with ropes, so that it could be drawn hither and thither in the theatre, and offered to the people of the highest rank.

The Water Theatre was still a sell-out in 1713, according to an announcement in the *Guardian* on 14 May:

> At the request of several persons of quality that came on Thursday last to the Mathematical Water Theatre of the late ingenious Mr Winstanley, when the house was full that they could not come in, this present day between 5 and 6 o'clock will be given to the spectator as before: 6 sorts of wine and brandy, to drink the Queen's health, all coming out of the barrel . . .

Three weeks earlier the same paper had listed the prices for admission: 'Box 2*s* 6*d*; Pit 2*s*; First Gallery 1*s* 6*d*; Upper Gallery 6*d*. Conveniences for coaches to be out of the way.' Another advertisement from the same period promised not only '6 several sorts of Wine', but also 'the best brandy and biskets, all coming out of the famous Barrel, and given to the Boxes and Pit; with Geneva [i.e. gin], Cherry beer, and Cyder to the first Gallery; there is also Coffee and Tea as at all other times'. There was further entertainment in the shape of 'Galathea's Flight from Polypheme, guided by two flying boys, with a flaming Torch playing Water through the Flames, a flying fiery Dragon, out of whose Mouth comes great Fire Balls . . . a large sheet of Water, with many Cascades of Water', and so on.

Although Winstanley was given the credit, the idea of the 'magic barrel' was far from new. In 1633 Henry van Etten describes a device that seems remarkably similar:

The vessell is thus made it must be divided into 3 sells for to contain the 3 liquors, which admit to Sacke,

Claret, and Whitewine. Now in the bung hole there is an Engine with 3 pipes, each extending to his proper sell, into which there is put a broach or funnell pierced in 3 places, in such sort that placing one of the holes right against the pipe which answereth into him, the other 2 pipes are stopped; then when it is full, turne the funnell, and then the former hole will be stopped and another open, to cast in other wine without mixing it with the other.

Now to draw out also without mixture, at the bottome of the vessell there must be placed a pipe or broach which may have three pipes and a cocke pierced with 3 holes so artificially done, that turning the cocke, the hole which answereth to such of the pipes that is placed at the bottom, may issue forth such wine as belongeth to that pipe, and turning the cocke to another pipe, the former hole will bee stopped, and so there will issue forth another kinde of wine without any mixture . . .

Winstanley had no monopoly on these devices: in 1710 a 'New Mathematical Fountain' was exhibited in the Black Horse Tavern in West Smithfield. John Ashton describes a 'Water Work, 12 Foot long and 9 foot high, made in white glass, in which is a

Tavern, a Coffee house, and a Brandyshop, which at your command runs at one Cock hot and Cold liquor, as Sack, Whitewine, Claret, Coffee, Tea . . . The like never performed in any Nation by any Person till Now.' In spite of this competition, Winstanley was the man who had introduced his contraption to the West End, and in the 1690s Winstanley's name was on everybody's lips. He was winning; he was becoming famous, and now he may well have believed that just one crowning achievement, one magnificent building, would be enough to guarantee him a place in history. Sir Christopher Wren had after all made himself immortal by means of bricks and mortar; Winstanley's former boss at Audley End, he had in death become a household name, to be remembered forever in the towering (though as yet incomplete) splendour of St Paul's Cathedral.

Although Wren was considerably more successful than Winstanley, there are a number of parallels between the two men. Like Winstanley, Wren had roots in the humble provinces; his father was a clergyman. Like Winstanley, Wren's first interests were not in building; at Westminster School he became proficient in Latin but, more notably, was fascinated by science and mathematics. When he was only twenty-five, he became Professor of Astronomy at Gresham College, London. A philosophical group of men, flourishing despite the vagabond nature which acquired for it the name of the 'Invisible College', gradually settled into two separate groups: those who met at Gresham College, and those who found London too distracting and preferred to congregate in Oxford. So one half would meet in Wren's rooms at Gresham College on the days when he had lectures there; the other half in rooms in Oxford, organized by Robert Boyle. After Charles II's restoration the Invisible College was able to make its outlines more tangible, and in mid-1662 the London group was incorporated by royal charter as the Royal Society.

Soon after its inauguration, Wren gave an address on what he considered the aims of this new Society: a myriad of them, from the study of meteorology and refraction to that of the growth of fruits and grain; plenty, scarcity and the price of corn; the seasons of fish, fowl and insects. All came under the modern trinity of knowledge, profit and convenience of life. Wren was a Fellow for twenty years, preserving this sort of ambitious pragmatism through a decade of scientific ingenuity, and into the architectural successes that were to make his name for posterity. It may have been one of his scientific achievements – the creation of a superb lunar globe – that prompted a surprise offer in 1661 to conduct an architectural survey of Tangier, a far harder project than mapping the moon – and one that he sensibly turned down.

Building and architecture were not isolated professions; architects were not, as Evelyn put it, 'mere illiterate mechanicks'. These occupations were closely wrapped up with science, all venerated as proofs of progress on a national level as they were in the mind of Charles II. Just as the king wanted impressive places to live in, he also wanted impressive scientific gadgets; Wren made some beautiful drawings of microscopic creatures for him; and Pepys, in a diary entry early in 1669, writes how he went down 'into the King's little elaboratory, under his closet, a pretty place; and there saw a great many chymical glasses and things, but understood none of them'. Charles may not have understood them either – but that was not the point. The point was to espouse technology.

In 1682 Denis Papin prepared a 'philosophical supper' for the President and Fellows of the Royal Society, where everything on the menu had been prepared in his newly invented 'digester' or pressure-cooker; in 1698 Thomas Savery took out the first steam engine patent; and in 1712 Thomas Newcomen built the first useful steam engine. The last quarter of the seventeenth century saw the scientific renaissance in turn give birth to the crucial technology of an evolving industrialized society. London was buzzing with this sort of practical science and technology; the capital was a tightly woven network of interdependent thinkers and experimenters. Winstanley was not really one of them, but they fed off and fostered a climate of development and daring which meant that people were receptive both to his clever gadgets and, later, to his fight to subdue nature with technology, just as others were doing.

Like Winstanley, most of these men were not one-trick ponies, constrained to specialize as scientists are now by sheer weight of knowledge. Wren became known as an architect, but he spent some time trying to solve the problem of longitude; Robert Hooke was primarily a scientist, but was also a surveyor and builder who helped in the reconstruction of the city after the Fire. In the halcyon days of his House of Wonders and his Waterworks, Winstanley was as enterprising as they were, even though he was not really interested in science beyond its capacity to entertain. But the ideas being dreamed up by members of the Royal Society were to shape his future. Or rather, in the case of the longitude problem, it was the ideas that were *not* being dreamed up that would shape it. As long as sailors could not tell where they were with any degree of accuracy or conviction, they were likely to come to grief – to run on to rocks like the Eddystone; and as long as ships kept sinking on rocks and reefs, there remained a desperate need for lighthouses to mark accident black spots and warn the sailors off.

One member of the royal commission to examine a plan for determining longitude at sea was John Flamsteed. He explained to the king that in principle it might be possible using the stars, but that the positions of the stars were not known with anything like enough accuracy. In response Charles decreed that he 'have them anew observed, examined, and corrected for the use of his seamen'. In 1675 he appointed Flamsteed Astronomical Observator by royal warrant; his job was 'forthwith to apply himself with the most exact care and diligence to the rectifying the tables of the motions of the heavens, and the places of the fixed stars, so as to find out the so much desired longitude of places for the perfecting of the art of navigation'. For this Flamsteed needed an observatory, and on the proceeds of the sale of some spoiled gunpowder, one was designed – by Christopher Wren – and hastily erected on the hill above the river at Greenwich. On this site, more than two hundred years later in 1884 – long after the solution had finally been found — was formally declared the defining line of longitude — 0 degrees: the Greenwich Meridian.

When Flamsteed first arrived, though, it was a lovely but useless observatory, its cement still drying and its interior empty of instruments. Just as Winstanley would have to pay for his lighthouse out of his own pocket, so Flamsteed was expected to buy his own astronomical instruments. He made some twenty thousand observations over the following twelve years, but because he could not afford the best equipment he excused them as being only preliminary and approximate. He was helped by the passionate meteorologist Richard Towneley, who provided Flamsteed with an escapement mechanism for a clock that would enable it to run for a whole year, so that he could find out whether the earth's rotation was regular.

While Flamsteed concentrated on mapping the stars of the northern hemisphere, Edmond Halley focused his attention on the south; instead of looking up at the night sky from the comfort of a custom-built observatory in the heart of London, he ventured to the remote island of St Helena in the southern Atlantic, abandoning his Oxford degree halfway through in his brave eagerness to turn his star-gazing addiction to some practical good. Halley stayed there in self-imposed exile for eighteen months, and though dogged by an unhelpful climate – the island seemed to be permanently cloudy, and he managed to chart only 341 stars – he made the first ever complete observation of the transit of the planet Mercury across the face of the sun. He returned to fame if not fortune, and was elected a member of the Royal Society at the tender age of twenty-two; he became secretary of the Royal Society in 1713 and later the second Astronomer Royal. Though now best known for the comet whose path he calculated and which is still called Halley's Comet, he also produced a map of ocean trade winds; investigated magnetic variation in 1698, producing a map of the results for navigators three years later; and made some impressive marine surveys.

At the same time as the nation's thinkers were trying to pin down more precisely the nature of things through science, debate raged in both England and France during the 1690s between the 'Ancients' and the 'Moderns', between the traditional philosophies of knowledge as epitomized by the Ancients, which were attacked by the opposition as ignorant, and the ideas of originality and progress that the Moderns felt characterized their own achievements. Winstanley, like Wren, would have considered himself a Modern: he was an innovator and he wanted to be saluted by future generations.

Wren's strain of ambition was similar to Winstanley's, though not quite as virulent; both were ruthless and both found fame by building on the misfortunes of others. Just as the destruction of London in the Great Fire of 1666 gave Wren his big chance, so centuries of shipwrecks raised the profile of Winstanley's challenge.

Wren's first city plan, scuppered by lack of cash and conflicting interests (much like the first Eddystone proposals), remains a record of his genius. But luckily he did not mind accepting second best – and indeed, since second best included a cathedral, fifty-two churches, thirty-six company halls, several private houses and a custom-house, he could hardly have complained about lack of challenge. St Paul's Cathedral took up years of his life, but Wren was knighted even before the first stone was laid; and the decades of delays did not diminish his stature as King's Surveyor, passionate, proprietorial and well known.

By the time Winstanley's attention was caught by Eddystone, the scientists of the Royal Society were involved in mapping the stars, and beginning to tackle the problem of longitude. The erection of a lighthouse was another way of reducing shipping losses – and it carried endorsement by the king. This was the kind of ambitious pragmatism, that combination of public gain and public fame, that Wren's Royal Society would have appreciated. And, just possibly, it might turn out to be Winstanley's ticket to eternal fame.

FIVE

OF SHIPS AND SHIPWRECKS

I saw her mainsail lash the sea
As I clung to the rock alone;
Then she heeled over, and down she went,
And sank like any stone.

By the mid-1690s Henry Winstanley was fifty-ish and a moderate success; he was beginning to make a name for himself. He had risen to a creditable position in the king's household at Audley End; he had learned the skill of engraving, and had made some money from an original set of playing cards; and he had built himself not only a fantastical house-cum-amusement-arcade in Essex but also a fabulous entertainment centre in London. He was looking for new places to invest his riches, and he bought a little fleet of five sailing ships.

This was a good time to buy. Entrepreneurs, especially in London, were now exploring and exploiting the benefits that science and technology could bring, but equally importantly they were experiencing the growth of commercial enterprise. Foreign trade was an important development in late seventeenth-century Britain, seen by many as unifying the nation. As one commentator eulogized in 1696, 'Trade is the Life Blood that runs through the Veins of the Nation, that moves, maintains, and enlivens the whole Body of the People from the meanest Cottage, to the Royal Throne.' Charles II had realized that it would be a good idea to buoy up this valuable national asset with constitutional incentives, and in 1660 he passed an 'Act for encouraging and increasing of shipping and navigation'.

This was supposed to help the British rival the Dutch in international trade, and to build up a solid base of merchant ships that would do as makeshift warships in emergencies. Previous Acts with similar aims had failed through being over-enthusiastic; a law that forbade all colonial trade and imports to England to all but English seamen simply could not be enforced, and had the effect of starving rather than nourishing trade. Now the prohibitions on 'alien' vessels were only partial. Compromise worked much better.

There were still deep-seated problems, however. One was the design of the ships themselves; compromise was needed here, too. Dutch 'flyboats' had proved to be an excellent trade-off between size and manoeuvrability: they had plenty of space for cargo, but were unarmed and therefore needed only small crews to man them. The English were good at both extremes – huge East Indiamen bristling with masts and cannons, and little coasters, nimble but unfit for the open seas. What was needed was a species of cheap ocean-going carrier with lots of room in the hold. George Downing, the MP and Exchequer official chiefly responsible for the new Navigation Act, scathingly described what the English were scraping by with as 'rather tubs than ships'.

Downing was the man who came up with another vital element of the new shipping strategies. He realized that, as the traditional trade routes with close European neighbours were slowly being saturated with competition, it was necessary to encourage trade with further-flung parts of Europe and, above all, to exploit the

American colonies which held supplies of wealth as yet largely untapped. His plan was to turn England into a sort of halfway-house between America and Europe, between supply and demand. The new Act allowed only English vessels to serve English colonies, and they could only go directly from England to the colony and back. A handful of other Acts passed soon afterwards refined the control, forcing English colonists to buy all their supplies from their motherland. England thus became a two-way depot, a warehouse where things could temporarily be stored while in transit either to the colonies or to continental Europe. Strange new substances were brought from America and India: spices, pepper, drugs, calicoes and chintzes from the Orient, tobacco and sugar from across the Atlantic. The English rapidly adopted new tastes and habits but, unable to consume all that arrived, also re-exported goods to Europe.

All this was clearly good news for sailors and shipbuilders; by a combination of the wartime appropriation of some of the coveted Dutch vessels and feverish activity in English dockyards, total tonnage doubled between the beginning and the end of Charles II's reign. The English now had the biggest merchant fleet in the world, and the most trained seamen too. Towns such as Plymouth were transformed by the new liveliness in trade. London was still the most important port by a long way, but the provinces were becoming ever more urbanized, as trade and industry made sophisticated city habits seem both more alluring and more accessible. Devon grew rich on the popularity of home-grown serges and 'stuffs' with their south- and east-European customers; though by the end of the century the cloths that were being brought back on the same boats – Turkish cotton, Spanish short wool – were much less in demand than their lightweight, brightly coloured Indian competitors. Tastes were changing; not only were people becoming richer, but they were abandoning tradition for modernity and spending their new money on novel commodities.

The gap between rich and poor was widening in both town and country, but where labour was in high demand, as in the ports, wages were rising, and so was disposable income. England's labourers were the envy of Europe: many could afford shoes; they rarely teetered on the breadline any more (or, if they did, it was probably the white breadline rather than the brown); some who had regular work now drank tea or coffee instead of beer, ate sugar instead of honey, and wore silk instead of wool. They bought more clocks and curtains and cutlery, though these 'durable goods' were often made rather to impress than to last.

Some feared the contagion of luxury and the corruption of greed that it might provoke among the lower classes; others, such as Sir Dudley North, a writer on economics, felt it a positive incitement to great achievement. 'The main spur to . . . Industry and Ingenuity', he wrote, 'is the exorbitant Appetites of Men, which they will take pains to gratifie, and so be disposed to work, when nothing else will incline them to it.' Winstanley's appetite for social status, which first spurred on his industrious and ingenious activities as engraver and showman, is a good case in point.

Investing in ships as Winstanley did was a popular way of making and losing fortunes; legends of enormous wealth spread and easily infected the new breed of money- and possession-hungry middle-class citizen with business aspirations. But as Winstanley and many others found out, buying a ship or two was not necessarily the way to get rich quick. There were too many unknown and uncontrollable factors for that. Wars, storms, pirates and rocks frequently messed up the merchants' plans. William of Orange's invasion of 1688 and the subsequent Revolution may have been 'gloriously' bloodless, but they threw the country into disorder in which random flux took a while to settle into positive progress.

The ongoing wars with France and Holland were good for naval dockyards and won more colonies, like the Canadian ones pilfered from France, but at the cost of a great many ships. Evelyn vividly describes the 'miserably shatter'd' remnants of the four-day battle of June 1666 limping into port with 'hardly a Vessel intire, but appearing rather so many wracks and hulls, so cruely had the *Dutch* mangled us . . .'. Predatory wartime privateers also disrupted both trade and civil engineering works such as Winstanley's. Winds were crucial and fickle: a gale could destroy a ship or blow her off course, while a flat calm could destroy her cargo if lack of wind meant it had to lie festering in a badly packed or rat-infested hold for weeks longer than planned. Transatlantic voyages were not becoming appreciably shorter, and as long as the problem of calculating longitude remained unsolved, and navigation therefore still inexact, vessels might easily take inadvertent detours, at best costly, at worst deadly.

Bankruptcy was more common in merchant shipping than in any other business, and merchants' fortunes were inseparable from those of sailors and shipowners, haulage and storage companies. This was a British Empire of trade, glued together not so much by patriotic ideology as by mercenary motives, and although it was big and powerful its very size also made it susceptible to outside influences – political, natural and criminal.

Henry Winstanley

In the late seventeenth century the Caribbean, the Mediterranean and the Indian Ocean were crawling with pirates. One of the most predatory of the sharks in the Caribbean was a Welshman, Captain Henry Morgan. He began with legitimate looting, taking part in a successful expedition in 1655 to seize Jamaica from the Spanish, and was promoted to second-in-command of the buccaneers plaguing the Dutch colonies in the Caribbean while the English were at war with them. He captured and ransacked settlements in Cuba and Venezuela and on the Isthmus of Panama, flexing his muscles before making the big push. In August 1670, with the help of two thousand buccaneers in thirty-six ships, he went for Panama itself, one of the strongholds of Spain's American empire. He demolished its formidable defences and looted the city while it burned to the ground.

Unfortunately for him, he had chosen the wrong moment to become aggressive. While England and Spain were at war, and the English watched angrily as the Spanish grew rich on the gold and silver which could have been theirs, Morgan and his mates were quietly encouraged to molest them at sea and on land. But this attack went far beyond molestation, and by the time he entered the city a peace treaty had already been signed between the English and the Spanish. Doing their best to seem shocked at his antics, the English authorities arrested him and sent him to London. Then the vicissitudes of international politics saw relations with Spain sour again, and Morgan's reputation was rescued — so much so that in 1674 the king knighted him for his rapacious services to the kingdom and made him Deputy Governor of Jamaica. Having become a respectable planter, Morgan lived and drank exorbitantly off the spoils of his crimes. The drink that finally killed him also gave him immortality: a brand of rum was named after him.

Morgan's reputation as a bloodthirsty pirate depends on an embellished account of his exploits by a Dutch member of his crew, but the truth was probably quite gory enough. His first ship, the *Oxford*, blew up and sank during an over-enthusiastic party on board, killing most of his guests but leaving Morgan alive to carry on thieving. He is known to have stolen from churches and to have stored his loot in some caves on the shore of Haiti. What is believed to have been Morgan's second ship, the *Jamaica Merchant*, recently discovered by a German treasure-hunter, sank off the coast of Haiti in the 1670s or '80s, probably hit by a hurricane.

Morgan's exploits were infamous, but there were plenty of other pirates eyeing up the merchants busy exploiting the West Indies, their ships full of goods just waiting to be appropriated. Most of the English settlers regarded the Caribbean islands as horrible places, fit only to assault, strip bare and leave for dead; Jamaica was characterized as being 'As Sickly as an Hospital, as Dangerous as the Plague, as Hot as Hell, and as Wicked as the Devil'. It was also 'Subject to Turnadoes, Hurricanes and Earthquakes'. The colonists shipped in African slaves to tend the sugar crops, and then worked both slaves and land to death. Since both slaves and sugar were in high demand, the vessels carrying them were prey to attack from both concerted foreign powers and solitary pirates. And neither of these groups would have had much more sympathy for the ship's crew than for their cargo, animate or inanimate.

Even as early as the thirteenth century, the port that was to become Plymouth was used as a meeting point for war-going fleets. With the increases in the town's wealth and in the number of ships came an increase in the number of undesirables. Stowe's *Annals*, in 1388, records that, 'certaine Pyrates sail about the havens of Cornwall and Devonshire, doing in all places much harme to the fishermen, and such shippes as they find unarmed they fiered. At length they entered Plimouth Haven where they brent certain great shippes and a great part of the towne.'

Records of shipwrecks in the area go back to 1362, when charges were made of illegal seizure of the spoils of the wreck of the *Tarrit*. There were plenty of other species of shipping parasites in addition to these indigenous terrors of the seas. In a vain attempt to discourage cross-Channel raids from Brittany, the townspeople stretched a chain boom across the mouth of the harbour; when this failed to keep out the marauders, they and the ships' crews had to flee into the countryside, saving their lives but sacrificing their ships and possessions. In 1640 nearby beaches were strewn with the remains of ships deliberately wrecked by their owners to prevent them falling into the clutches of the enemy. Sometimes Turks, Algerians and Tunisians even scavenged the coastal towns for galley slaves; hapless captives had to rely on the chance of an altruistic or short-staffed captain happening to sail past and agreeing to pay the ransom money. One of the terms of a treaty signed in 1662 with Algeria was that all British slaves in Algiers should be paid for at their market price and set free, and that no more should be captured; who was to finance this was unclear – Charles II was continuously short of cash, and it probably never happened.

It was to guard against not only external dangers to the town but internal ones too that Plymouth's Citadel was built. Three years after the foundation stone was laid in 1666, Count Magalotti, who was employed by an Italian prince to travel round

Europe with him and take notes, wrote that the Citadel was 'built by the king to be a check on the inhabitants, who showed themselves on former occasions prone to sedition, and that spirit being now fostered by the influx of wealth which a flourishing commerce produces, renders them objects of reasonable suspicion'. It was to be 'a defence to the port against the sea, hence it equally commands the sea, or the town, and defends or batters, as occasion may require'. The threat of home-grown pirates on the Devon coast was only too real; in 1579 a partnership of Scottish merchants complained to the Crown that, 'a month before, a ship of theirs, laden with sundry merchandise was despoiled at Torquay by one John Grainger of Plymouth, and one Captain Morrice, along with sixty other English pirates'.

These human dangers were bad enough, but the sailors faced natural perils too. They had always to contend with bad weather, strong eddying currents and hidden rocks. Plymouth had more than its fair share of off-putting features, which made it a slow developer as a major port. The wide sweep of the Sound, hollowed out over millennia by currents from the estuaries of four Devon rivers, creates a natural anchorage that makes Plymouth unique; but while it provides better shelter than anywhere else, it can also act as a trap. When the wind blows onshore sailing ships have great difficulty getting out, which is one reason why generations of captains preferred to use other estuaries nearby.

The primary cause of wrecks was the elements; collisions owing to congestion, especially after Plymouth was promoted to the major naval base of the south-west by the Admiralty in 1690, came a close second. Trailing in joint third place were fire, explosion, accident and enemy action. In 1637, according to State Papers, the *Paulsgrove*, a London ship heading for home, was greeted by the onset of an unexpected storm as she left her moorings. The crew tried to persuade the captain to turn back, but 'being in a fretful mood and passionate humour, [he] threwe down his staff and stamping said, that he would not return'. His men gave up pleading with him; there seemed more point in pleading with God for mercy now. An hour later they were stopping holes and baling out, and soon afterwards the ship was driven ashore.

Gradually, attempts were made to improve safety. As a direct result of the sinking in 1691 of the *Harwich*, a 70-gun naval vessel, lost with all 420 of her crew, buoys were installed to mark the safe channels between the rocks and reefs. But these were not enough. Ships still sank, and when they did there was no organized way of rescuing the survivors. There was no lifeboat in Plymouth until 1803, and the first two that were put in service only sat in their boathouses until they were claimed by harbour authorities with more initiative.

Despite all the troubles of life on the ocean, those who led such lives were numerous and often influential, by status or by weight of numbers. Britain felt more than ever like a maritime nation. Downstream from London Bridge all one could see, as the writer John Macky put it, was 'a continued Forest of Ships of all Nations', and although sailors probably made up only 5 or 10 per cent of the population in major ports, they made their presence felt. From her fleeting visit to Plymouth Celia Fiennes had the impression that the town was 'mostly inhabitted with seamen and those which have affaires on the sea'. This was not really the case – there were plenty of other sorts of people in the town – but the sea and seamen made up some of the boldest-coloured threads of the fabric of English life.

A maritime survey carried out in 1619 counted in Plymouth 604 mariners (17 per cent of Devon's total population!) and 57 ships, with a total tonnage of just over 3,000 tons (31 per cent of the county's total). Those who returned safe from their voyages brought back money, foreign delicacies and tales of adventure; those who did not were missed and mourned. Merchants and shipowners often worked their way into politics; reports on the arrivals of ships took up columns of space in the newspapers.

In the smoky corners of the proliferating coffee-houses, not only were tea and coffee and hot chocolate consumed in huge and sugary quantities, but rumours were spread, opinions aired, deals struck, and friendships made and broken. 'They smoak, game, and read the *Gazettes*, and sometimes make them too. Here they treat of Matters of State, the Interests of Princes, and the Honour of Husbands, &c. In a Word, 'tis here the *English* discourse freely of every Thing, and where they may be known in a little Time.' In these establishments shipping merchants would hear about loads to be bid for, or the misfortune of a fellow trader attacked by a pirate at sea. Reputations were made and lost. Winstanley's Waterworks would have had their most valuable publicity through word of mouth; his later fame would have spread in the same way. The benefits were mutual: as the coffee-houses supported sea trade, so Winstanley's lighthouse was to facilitate it.

The cafés and the ships were linked directly by tea and coffee and sugar, but also, less directly, by financiers. The money men had realized that the huge risks inherent in shipping could be turned to profit, could be calculated and reduced to figures. Fire insurance was born in the 1680s, but did not prosper as the slightly more mature marine

The English Coffee-House

The first English coffee-house was opened in 1650 in Oxford; two years later Londoners followed suit, and soon the whole country was infested. Admission generally cost a penny, and coffee was still relatively expensive, so the clientele, as well as being literate and almost entirely male, was solvent, though not necessarily exclusive. Inevitably men of different professions and political persuasions came together at particular haunts. Steele's *London Gazette* mocked the tendency: 'All accounts of Gallantry, Pleasure, and Entertainment, shall be under the Article of *White's Chocolate-house*; Poetry, under that of *Will's Coffee-house*; Learning, under the title of *Grecian*; Foreign and Domestic News, you will have from the *St. James's Coffee-house* . . .'

Coffee-houses often doubled up as libraries and debating chambers, being provided with periodicals, the latest polemical best-sellers, and customers to pass passionate judgement on them. Swift writes of the 'Committees of Senators who are silent in the House, and loud in the Coffee-house, where they nightly adjourn to chew the cud of politics, and are encompassed with a ring of disciples who lie in wait to catch up their droppings.' Members of the Royal Society frequented them, and intellectual developments were discussed alongside social scandal and religious upheaval. Addison, whose career path wound between literature and politics, was 'ambitious to have it said of me, that I have brought Philosophy out of Closets and Libraries, Schools and Colleges, to dwell in Clubs and Assemblies, at Tea-Tables, and in Coffee-Houses'.

Pepys spent many an evening in them; in February 1664 he records that, 'In Covent Garden tonight I stopped at the great Coffee-house [later Wills'], where I never was before; where Dryden the poet (I knew at Cambridge), and all the wits of the town, and Harris the player, and Mr. Hoole of our College [i.e. Gresham]. And had I time then, or could at other times, it will be good coming thither; for there I perceive is very witty and pleasant discourse.'

insurance market did. One of the biggest names in the business, Edward Lloyd, gave the two hundred or so faceless underwriters more of an identity when in 1680 he founded a coffee-house where they could meet shipowners, captains and merchants, who could be encouraged to sell their souls with complimentary cups of coffee; thus was born Lloyds of London.

Winstanley presumably did not know about these new insurance brokers, or else he decided to place his trust in Providence rather than in upstart businessmen; if he had chosen Man over God and insured his ships he might not have felt their loss so keenly. In the event, it was not in the recently established coffee-house of Edward Lloyd but in a London pub that Winstanley heard the news that his ships had gone down on Christmas Eve in 1695. His anger drove him to Devon and to realize the desperate need for a lighthouse. But, unlike many others who had lost ships, it also drove him to action.

TO BUILD A LIGHTHOUSE

*To give light to them that sit in darkness and in
the shadow of death . . .*

Before Winstanley came along, no one had ever
tried to build a lighthouse on a bare rock in the
open sea. However, for at least two thousand years
people had constructed lighthouses at the entrance
to harbours, to guide ships in, and on rocky
promontories to warn them off. For Winstanley,
these were encouraging precedents, but was it
really possible to construct a lighthouse on the
Eddystone?

The most famous of all lighthouses, one of the
Seven Wonders of the ancient world, was in Egypt.
Alexander the Great became King of Macedonia
before he was twenty, and he was a born leader.
Taught by Aristotle, he was a great scholar and
helped promote Greek knowledge and culture far
beyond the geographical boundaries of Greece.
Sculptors elevated the king to almost superhuman

status by exploiting romantic images of him as an explorer of the unknown and an exceptional statesman. When he founded the city of Alexandria at the mouth of the Nile in 332 BC, he ordered that a great breakwater, a mile long, should be built out from the shore to the little island of Pharos, thus partly enclosing the east harbour as a safe haven for ships. He further decreed that, to guide sailors to the harbour, a colossal tower should be built on the island, and that in the hours of darkness a fire should burn on top of the tower, so that it would be visible by night as well as by day, advertising his great new metropolis around the clock.

And so it was done – though it took a long time to finish. Upon the death of Alexander the Great in 323 BC, one of his generals, Ptolemy I, obtained control of Egypt, but it was only during the reign of his successor, the second Ptolemy, that the lighthouse is thought to have been completed. On the site now occupied by the medieval citadel Ptolemy erected a limestone tower, 450 feet high – half the height of the Eiffel Tower or the Empire State Building. Indeed, it remained the tallest roofed structure ever built until it was over-shadowed by twentieth-century American skyscrapers.

The lighthouse was made up of three sections, like an implausible tower made from a child's wooden building-blocks: at the bottom, a truncated pyramid; balanced on that, a pyramidal octagon; finally a circular section topped by the lantern. It was probably equipped with internal lifts to haul the fuel to the top, to feed the hungry fire which could be seen from 40 miles out to sea. To this day no taller lighthouse has been built, nor one more awe-inspiring than this gleaming white tower, crowned with an imposing bronze statue of Neptune. The Arabian geographer Edrisi visited it in the thirteenth century, and it seems from what he says of it that the lighthouse had not aged much during the previous one and a half millennia:

> This lighthouse has not its equal in the world for excellence of construction and for strength, for not only is it constructed of a fine quality stone, called 'kedan', but the various blocks are so strongly cemented together with melted lead, that the whole is

imperishable, although the waves of the sea continually break against its northern face; a staircase of the ordinary width, constructed in the interior, extends as high as the middle of the structure, where there is a gallery; under the staircase are the keepers' apartments; above the gallery the tower becomes smaller and smaller until it can be embraced by the arms of a man. From the same gallery there is a staircase much narrower than the tower, reaching to the summit; it is pierced by many windows to give light within and to show those who ascend where to place their feet. At a distance the light appeared so much like a star near the horizon that sailors were frequently deceived by it.

Sadly the 'imperishable' whole was soon to prove its admirer wrong; it survived until 1302, but then, its light having burned unwaveringly through the fickle flux of so many peoples and empires, the tower was destroyed by an earthquake, its demise perhaps hastened by the ruthless invasion of the Ottoman armies.

A fun but far-fetched story that clings to the construction of the lighthouse has it that the architect Sostratus carved his name into the outer

Henry Winstanley, self-portrait. This oil painting hangs in the Saffron Walden Museum, and shows Winstanley as a slightly immature character of perhaps thirty, with a hint of a roguish smile and a glint in his eye. (*Saffron Walden Museum*)

Saffron Walden church with Winstanley's spire and lanthorn (between the lower spires).

(Saffron Walden Library)

Winstanley House, The Cock-Pit, Saffron Walden, a few yards from the library and market place. Henry is believed to have been born here in March 1644. (*Adam Hart-Davis*)

Overleaf: Four of Winstanley's playing cards. The king of hearts shows Charles II with his wife in front of the Thames and London Bridge, plus the monument put up by Christopher Wren and Robert Hooke to commemorate the Great Fire of 1666. Other cards show fanciful representations of people in 'national costume'. (*Collection of the Worshipful Company of Makers of Playing Cards, Guildhall Library, London*)

♥ KING

LONDON

ENGLISH

England, and Scotland, are two Kingdoms Unto the Title of Great Britain, are united, though not the greater the most considerable in the War for Riches, Plenty, Strength &c: England has many Kings. it contains 52 Shires or Countys under the principle of Wales but it is 40 Bishopricks, an Cambridge York & the Rivers of Tamus severn & Humber are very Considerable. Scotland there is two Arch-Bishopricks at St Andrews, and Glasgow, Bishopricks, Edenborough is the capital City near to Which the Tea Port Leith here is also two Universities. Aberdeen & Glasquo and the Chief Rivers in this Country is the Tay, but towards the West is the Kingdom of Ireland, an Arch-Bishoprick on the Crown of England, here are two Arch-Bishopricks, Armagh Dublin &c: Dublin is the Capital of that Kingdom and Seat of the Vice King and the chief University, here is also 19 Bishopricks, and Cork Limerick Drogdah &c: are good Citys and Sea Ports and the chief Rivers is the Shenton this Country with England lys between the 50 & 60 deg: North Lat: and 8 & 21 long and is Generally Called the British Isles Plantations See New England

★ ACE

AME   RICA

I ♣

America so Called from Americus Vespusius who Discovered some Parts of it but it was first found out by Christopher Columbus of Genoa in the Year 1486 at the charge of Ferdinand King of Aragon & Castile, and therefore it was given wholly to the Spaniards by Pope Alexander the 6th but the Europeans not Consenting to lose a Part of so great a Prize had Planted some Colonys though all Counted together are not so Considerable as what the Spaniards Possess in it who Called the New World so greatly & for its being so largely known to us, though for many Regions thought by some to be known to the Antient in Part in whole and by Mariners its Generally Called the West Indie by reason of its Situation that way from us to be distinguished from the Other India Before this Discovery it Contained the two great Empires of Mexica & of Peru whose glory & magnificence, if Considered we should Lament their Ignorance of a True Deity and their falling under the Tyranny of the Spaniards that has Destroyed so many Millions of them.

ACE

AFRICK

Africk is a Peninsula Joyned to Asia
by a narrow Isthmus bounded on the East by the
Red Sea & bay of Arabia, On the North With the
Mediterranean sea, and on the west & south
with the Atlantick & Ethiopick Ocean. it is
much bigger then Europe & lesser then Asia
but less Peopled & fruitful then Either & Was
little discovered by the Ancients except towards
the North which passed under the name of Libya,
it is equally seated under the Equator advancing
Either ways Near 36 degrees therefore most
under the Torrid Zone here is all the generation
of the Moors supposed to be the off spring of
Ham who was cursed of his father Noah: here are
many Idolaters, Mahomitans & slum Christian
Colonys. here are found most Monsters & variety
of strange Beasts

V

AGRA

MONGVLS

The Empire of the Great Mongul is the main Land of
India & many Tributary Kingdoms on the coast. There
a Tribe of Tartars Planted here by the Mighty Tamerlane
and now the most Absolute Monarch may be Esteemed
one of the Greatest & Richest Emperors of the World in
Gold Pretious stones Elephants & the Domine over many
then & Kingdoms whose great nations are Generally
from its Chief City Agra, Isg, & Lahor, are, not only
Capital of their Kingdom But where this Emperor
has 3 Magnificent Palace & some Temples Covered with
Gold Cusbud, Candahar, Caçimir, Dulbinda, Mandao,
Pengab, Siba, Cambaia, Jangapur, arate, Bangala &
which are very Considerable. Kingdoms & City of
this Empire. Jenkhaia & Bangala are great Sea Ports
for where the English has a Factory, Amadabad Brother
Brochia, Faepore, Goa, Diu & also Diu belonging to the Portugal:
Keckmer & Her, famous for its Idol the Mecque.
People are Most Idolaters, The Emperor & Nobles, Maha
metans but of late here are some Christian Churches.

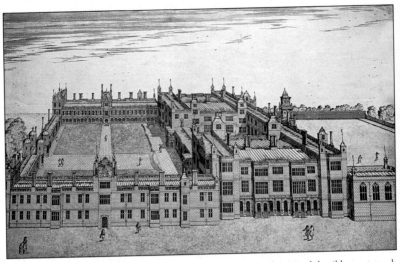

One of Winstanley's engravings of Audley End, showing fine architectural detail but not much artistic skill. Only the central part still stands. (*Saffron Walden Museum*)

'The morning', one of Henry Winstanley's artistic creations, which shows what he probably imagined was a typical scene in an upper-class household. (*Saffron Walden Museum*)

Audley End as it is today. After its 'improvement' in the early seventeenth century the house had four extra wings, each about the size of the central chunk, which is all that remains. The River Cam flows past the front of the house, and the beautiful walled garden is just to the left of the picture. (*Adam Hart-Davis*)

Christopher Wren. For a short time he was Winstanley's boss at Audley End, and certainly he was a profound influence upon him, for Winstanley reckoned that he might become famous by designing buildings, just as Wren had. (*National Portrait Gallery*)

Winstanley's House of Wonders at Littlebury, on the main Cambridge road, and opposite the church. Note the windmill in the back garden, the 'lanthorn' on the roof and the turnstile in the front fence. (© *Copyright The British Museum*)

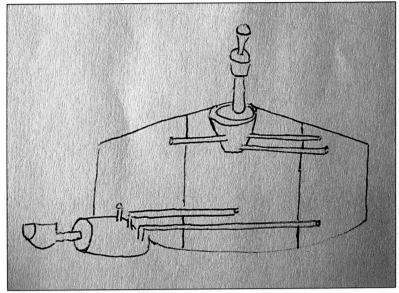

The mechanism of the 'magic barrel' described by van Etten in 1633 (see p. 60) – Winstanley's barrel was probably a more complex version of this. The barrel is divided into three compartments, or cells. When liquid is poured into the top funnel, a secret twist of the inlet tube would direct the liquid into the correct cell. Likewise a secret twist of the stopcock bottom left would allow delivery of the chosen liquid. (*Hazel Forsyth*)

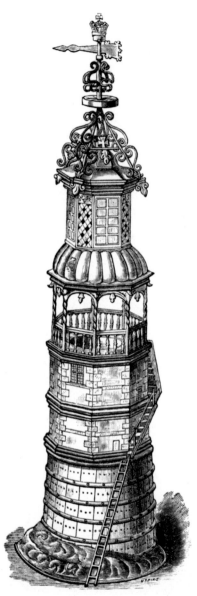

Henry Winstanley commissioned this elegant solid silver salt (salt-cellar) from the well-known Plymouth goldsmith Peter Rowe, and said it had cost more than £90 – a vast sum of money in 1698. It stands 19 inches high and is an exact copy of the 1698 lighthouse, right down to the outside ladder and staircase.

(*City of Plymouth Museums & Art Gallery*)

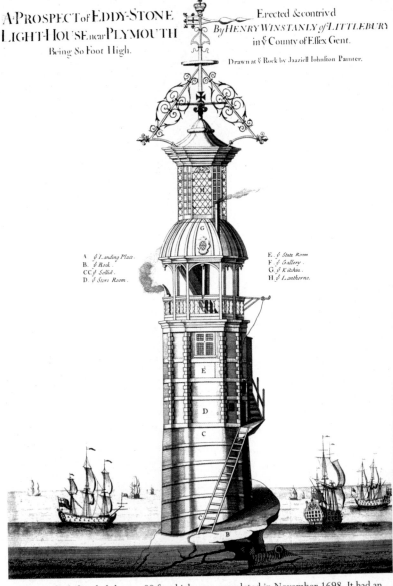

A PROSPECT of EDDY-STONE LIGHT-HOUSE near PLYMOUTH

Being 80 Foot High.

Erected & contriv'd By HENRY WINSTANLY of LITTLEBURY in y.e County of Essex Gent.

Drawn at y.e Rock by Jaaziell Johnston Painter.

A . y.e Landing Place .
B . y.e Rock .
CC y.e Sollid .
D . y.e Store Room .

E . y.e State Room
F . y.e Gallery .
G . y.e Kitchin .
H . y.e Lanthorne.

Winstanley's first lighthouse, 80 feet high, was completed in November 1698. It had an outside ladder and staircase, and a colossal wrought-iron bracket above to carry the weather-vane. He lit the candles on 14 November, but the weather became so bad that he was then marooned on the lighthouse for five weeks. (*Heritage-Images/Science Museum, London*)

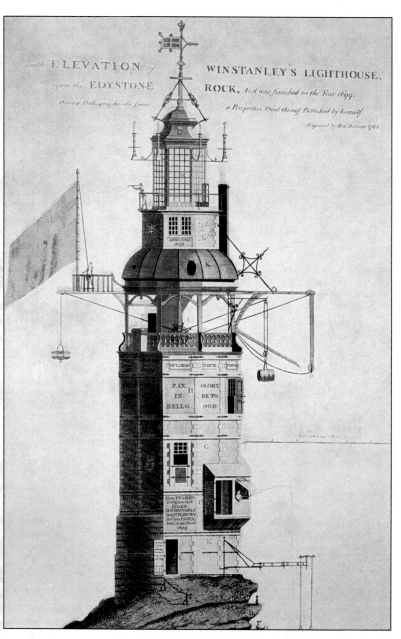

The final version of Winstanley's lighthouse – decorated, flamboyant and 100 feet high – as it would have been when he was in it for the Great Storm of 1703.

(© Copyright The British Museum)

Adam and crew in a rowing boat, as close to the elements as Winstanley must have been, on their way back from the Eddystone rock, shown right, with Smeaton's Stump, and the current Eddystone Lighthouse (see p. 196). Note that at high tide only two rocks are visible. (*Paul Bader*)

wall, and then covered it with a layer of mortar into which he cut an inscription giving the credit for the building to Ptolemy. His idea was that the flimsy false testimony in the mortar would in time crumble away to reveal to posterity the name of the true designer. His plan sort of worked for, writing about the tower a few hundred years later, Pliny the Younger comments, 'I cannot but note the singular magnanimity of kind Ptolemy, who permitted Sostratus of Gnidus to grave his own name in this building.' His name survived longer than Ptolemy's in stone, if not in history.

Just as the Eddystone Lighthouse was named after the rocks on which it was built, so the lighthouse of Alexandria, built on the island of Pharos, came to be called the Pharos, and this word still lingers as a generic term for lighthouse in the Romance languages: in Italian, Spanish and Portuguese it is *faro*, and in French *phare*. But although the construction of the Pharos was a great achievement, the problems were in various ways more easily soluble than those at Eddystone.

The Pharos foundations were built on dry bedrock, many feet above high tide, and there was a causeway from the mainland along which the workforce could commute and bring the building materials.

The Roman approach to providing coastal warnings was predictably functional. Expanding their empire with efficiency and little time for aestheticism, they erected a series of serviceable but not very spectacular beacon-towers as far west as Dover and Boulogne. At Dover they built a lighthouse on each side of the harbour, to guide their ships in the dark — and, it is said, to encourage nervous legionaries waiting in Gaul to embark on their first sea voyage. The eastern tower still survives, or at least the bottom 40 feet of it does, topped by 20 feet of medieval upper storey, and surrounded by the walls of the medieval castle. This Roman tower, dating from the second century AD, can claim the title of the oldest lighthouse in England. By the time the Roman Empire began to decline towards the end of the fifth century, there were at least thirty lighthouses in regular operation. Then civilization began to succumb to barbarism: buildings were knocked down rather than created; the axe and the sword were wielded instead of the pen; Roman laws were flouted rather than obeyed.

As trust dried up, so did trade; shipbuilding and lighthouses were replaced by piracy. The coastal lights which had once been friendly warnings were now distrusted, and flickered out one by one. Europe was submerged in the Dark Ages. Lighthouses reverted to the primitivism of bonfires, and only when the chaos began to die down and trade to pick up again did their long evolutionary process restart as if from scratch. The first few steps were taken with the aid of the few religious survivors of the centuries of darkness. The Romans, who had brought civilization, had also introduced Christianity, and it was the Christians who now began to make things civilized again.

Before the Reformation, monks on St Michael's Mount near Land's End in Cornwall used to light fires in a stone lantern known as St Michael's Chair

– right on top of the tower – for the benefit of local fishermen, and a beacon was lit there when the Spanish Armada hove into view in 1588. On the bank of the Humber in the fifteenth century a rich-man-turned-hermit put a lantern on top of the tower in which he was living, and it carried on radiating its warning for two hundred years.

One shining example of maritime architecture was to be found at Cordouan in western France. Here, in the seventeenth century, only eighty years before Winstanley began to take an interest in the Eddystone, work was completed on a lighthouse built on rocks only barely above the high-water mark. The Bay of Biscay was well known among sailors for much the same reasons as the entrance to Plymouth Sound. An anomaly in the sea bed, here a deep cleft in the rock rather than a towering spire, confuses the currents, creating lethal and opposing swells. There is an estuary near Bordeaux whose mouth is wide but filled with teeth of rock and shoals, one of which is the islet of Cordouan, a rocky platform that is all but submerged at high tide.

To Build a Lighthouse

Ever since the ninth century traders have been attracted to Bordeaux by its fine wines, but scared off by its perilous natural approach; from as early as 880 AD a beacon of sorts is known to have existed on Cordouan in response to shippers' complaints and the danger of their beneficial trade being diverted elsewhere. A structure that could be classed as a lighthouse first appeared when the area became an English province, ruled over by Edward the Black Prince. Bloodthirsty soldier he may well have been, but he did succeed in getting a 48-foot lighthouse built; he also found the perfect person to live on the rock and look after it – a religious hermit. He also set up one of the earliest systems of lighthouse dues, and charged each passing boat 2 groats.

The first recorded grant in Britain to collect lighthouse dues was accorded to the Barons of the Cinque Port of Winchelsea in 1261 and gave them the right 'that from every ship putting into the port of Winchelsea, laden with merchandise, they shall take 2d for the maintenance of a light which they shall have in their port for the safety of sailors putting in there by night'. This set a trend which was to be followed for centuries; since it was hardly practicable to demand cash from a ship sailing past an isolated tower, the claim for a toll to cover the running costs of the tower became part of the vessel's welcome into harbour. One exception to the mercenary norm was in Kent, where in 1367 sailors were encouraged by the Church to pay their dues with the offer of indulgences if they would support the 'poor hermit, Brother Nicholas de Legh of the hermitage of St Margaret's Strait, Kent'; they would receive not only a guiding light for their coppers, but also a forty-day remission of temporal punishment.

In 1409 the hermit-keeper of the light on Cordouan made an application to Henry IV, then ruler of the area, to double his dues in order to repair some storm damage; the request was granted and he was allowed to relieve the captains of all the ships leaving Bordeaux groaning under the weight of wine of twice as many coins as before. It seems likely, however, that in general more of these groats found their way into the pocket of the Black Prince and those who followed him than into his hermit's, financing the ruler's lifestyle more generously than the lighthouse service. This may help to explain why the stream of successors to the original hermit eventually dried up completely. Although the islet had since become home to a small fishing community, the tower was abandoned and remained so until the wine merchants once again became irritated enough, towards the end of the sixteenth century, to demand a replacement.

The Parisian architect Louis de Foix, who took on the job of reconstruction, wanted to impress more than to save lives. At the top of a lavish combination of palace, cathedral and fortress was hung a lantern which looked like an afterthought. The islet which in the Black Prince's time had been attached to the mainland had by now been separated from it by two hundred years of the sea's erosion. It still disappeared at high water, and even at low water there was only one shingle beach along all of its thousand-yard length where a boat could be safely landed.

The construction of just the round base took several years; then de Foix's fun really started. He made a 'wedding-cake' structure of four cylindrical storeys of diminishing size. The largest was 50 feet in diameter and was where the four keepers were to live. Above them was the King's Apartment, a gorgeous suite of rooms in which no monarch seems to have been sufficiently sensible – or adventurous – to take a weekend break. One level closer to God was a chapel with a domed mosaic ceiling. Perched above this were the emergency and the everyday lantern rooms. Everywhere there were carvings and arches and gilded decoration. Clearly, de Foix must have expected both that sailors would dare to take their eyes from the rock-infested waters, and that they would recognize and be interested in the catalogue of neo-classical pillars that he erected around the ground floor – the first Doric, the next Ionic, the third Corinthian, the fourth his own original mixture.

Twenty-seven years passed between the commissioning of the new lighthouse at Cordouan and its completion. Something simpler might have been quicker, and would have better served the wine-sellers of the time, but it would never have had such grandeur or such romance, or have earned the title the Patriarch of Lighthouses. And it would never have inspired the lighthouse builders of the future in the same way. The extensive and solid natural foundation of Cordouan and its proximity to the land gave the architect a relatively straightforward task – at least compared to that which faced Winstanley – but its magnificence made the possibility of Winstanley's success seem a little less remote.

The coasts of Winstanley's Britain were far from featureless. There were already a few lighthouses, and, more significant and useful at the time, there was an abundance of natural sea-marks. Mariners would trust their inadequate, inaccurate charts only as far as was necessary to get them in sight of the land, where they could revert to the more trustworthy evidence of their eyes. Far more reassuring than scribbles on parchment were the familiar signposts of the English coastline – the strange and well-known shape of a rock, the profile of a headland, the clumps of trees by day or lights by night, the brightly painted white house or the church spire. These markers were as indispensable as they were informal, and in 1566 Elizabeth I made official what was already generally accepted, that they must not be removed or altered:

> Forasmuch as by the destroying and taking away of certain steeples, woods and other marks standing upon the main shores of the sea coasts adjoining to this realm of England and Wales being as beacons and marks of ancient time accustomed for seafaring men . . . divers ships . . . have by the lack of such marks of late years been miscarried, perished and lost in the sea . . .

Anyone who did so would have to pay a £100 fine or be immediately outlawed. Whenever a valuable marker was accidentally damaged its repair was a top priority for Trinity House.

The Brethren of Trinity House had been set up by Henry VIII as part of his reform of naval warfare. As well as providing his ships with good enough guns and making them agile enough to outmanoeuvre the Spanish fleet, which far outnumbered them, the king established a Navy Board to deal with the important administrative trifles that the Lord Admiral might have considered beneath him, and thus ensured that every component of his defences remained well-oiled. Then, in 1512, he gave a group of master mariners in Deptford leave to form a guild 'in honour of the Holy Trinity and Saint Clement' (a martyr drowned by being thrown into the sea tied to an anchor, considered by some to be the patron saint of sailors). This guild was formalized two years later as the 'Brotherhood of the Most Glorious and Undividable Trinity' and the 'Brethren and Sisters of the same'. They had 'power and authority' to do whatever they saw fit 'for the relief, increase and augmentation of the shipping of this our Realm of England'. The 1566 Act of Elizabeth referred to above authorized them not only to see to the reparation of natural sea-marks, but also to take the initiative in their reinforcement with artificial ones: 'from time to time . . . and at their costs to make, erect, and set as such and so many beacons, marks, and signs for the sea, in such place or places of the sea-shores, and uplands near the sea-coasts . . . as to them shall seem most needful and requisite, whereby the dangers may be avoided and escaped, and ships the better come into their ports without peril . . .'.

Nevertheless, the authority of Trinity House as far as lighthouses were concerned was doomed to a long and inconclusive battle against royalty and private enterprise. Rich men wanted to make themselves richer by building often inadequate or unnecessary lighthouses and charging sailors often extortionate dues for passing them; after relinquishing some of the profits to the monarch, they would pocket the rest. Trinity House would protest that they had a monopoly on lighthouse construction and that sailors' welfare was being compromised by beacons erected for personal gain. Samuel Pepys, appointed Elder Brother and in two separate years (1676 and 1699) Master of Trinity House, was one who condemned 'the evil of having lights raised for the profit of private men, not for the good of the public seamen, their widows and orphans'.

To Build a Lighthouse

Pepys devoted himself to the cause of nationalized versus privatized control, though his diaries are peppered with some spicy irreverences: he refers to the Brethren as a whole as 'the old sokers' and to one in particular as a 'lazy, corrupt, doating Rogue'. On one occasion he writes reprovingly, 'I found them reading their Charter which they did like fools, only reading here and there a bit, whereas they ought to do it all, every word . . .'. In 1661 Pepys was approached by prospective lighthouse builder Captain Murford, who offered him one-eighth of the profits if he would support his application; the fact that he writes of this seems good evidence that Pepys did not accept the bribe. This sort of practice must have been disillusioning; and the *Naval Minutes* seem to indicate that the state of affairs in the 1680–3 period was dismal enough to sap his conviction altogether: 'Even the Trinity House is grown corrupt and useless!'

Pepys might just have been having a bad day when he wrote this, but Trinity House, if not corrupt and useless, was certainly conservative and negative. The cat-fighting with entrepreneurs which was supposed to prevent the exploitation of sailors, combined with a Civil War which was hardly conducive to foreign trade or investment in aids to trade, resulted in a very sparse sprinkling of lighthouses. By the end of the seventeenth century, just as Winstanley was preparing to enter the arena, there were only fifteen around the whole coastline of England and Wales, mostly still privately owned and ineffective, as many owners were trying to cut corners by skimping on expensive fuel.

The Brethren of Trinity House had philanthropic reasons to discourage the building of lighthouses – they wanted to prevent the construction of useless ones – but a substantial number of other people, motivated by selfishness and inhumanity, had the same goal; these were the wreckers, for whom shipwrecks provided not only a living but a way of life. Wrecking is as old as the shipping upon which it feeds: after a shipwreck the Greeks and Romans would appropriate the cargo and sell the crew as slaves; in fifteenth- and sixteenth-century Britain attackers preferred merely to steal the goods, and to kill anyone left alive, since superstition held that they would bring bad luck if they lived; furthermore some say Cornish custom was that the cargo belonged to any survivors . . .

Tales of wreckers are perfect fodder for over-imaginative storytellers, but there is no doubt that all around the coast of Britain there were lights replacing or being added to those of legitimate lighthouses – even being tied to horses' tails to simulate the swinging lights of ships – to lure vessels towards what appeared to be safe havens, but were in fact rocks where looters lurked. After a particularly lucrative incident, when the ship *John and Lilley* was wrecked on the Devon coast, a local poet wrote a celebratory song, which began,

> The *John and Lilley* came ashore
> To feed the hungry and cloathe the poor.

Perhaps he was compensated for his creative exertions with a keg or two of rum by the self-proclaimed Robin Hoods of the sea. Cornwall is more renowned for its wreckers than any other part of Britain, and Cornishman Sir John Killigrew's exploits of 1619 helped to give the county its reputation. He started with good intentions to build a lighthouse on Lizard Point, and ask only for voluntary contributions from passing ships. Not only did he have to fight long and hard against Trinity House, who said the light would be of no use and would only attract enemies, but when he had finally obtained the grant he found he could not obtain local labour or materials. The locals did not want to do anything that might prevent ships from encountering the treacherous coastline, thus spoiling their nice little earner. Killigrew bitterly translates their objections: 'They affirm I take away God's grace from them. Their English meaning is that now they shall receive no more benefit by shipwreck, for this will prevent it. They have been so long used to reap profit by the calamities of the ruin of shipping, that they claim it to be hereditary.'

Killigrew did build his lighthouse, but he made enemies on both land and sea, for captains declared, when the dues were made compulsory to cover costs, that they had no intention of paying for a light which failed to work properly. So he abandoned his troublesome philanthropy and defected to the opposition. Eight years later he had his own gang of wreckers and like his former enemies was claiming wreckers' rights 'through custom and descent'.

In this maritime world of vested interests it was usually the common sailor who came off worst. As Secretary at the Naval Office, Pepys complained of how difficult it was to find ships and sailors willing to go to war in them: 'Horrible trouble with the backwardness of the merchants to let us have their ships, and seamen's running away, and not to be got or kept without money.' He regrets that it is necessary to 'presse seamen, without which we cannot really raise men'. Only later does he admit that these sailors were not greedy but wretched, 'that the desperate condition that we put men into for want of their pay makes them mad, they being as good men as ever were in the world, and would as readily serve the King again were they but paid'.

Sailors wanted to avoid being press-ganged into service not only because they were badly treated but also because they were badly paid, or sometimes not paid at all. Cromwell's enthusiasm for colonial wars had resulted in huge accumulated wages owed to crews, debts which he left to his successor. Charles II's idea was to pay them off with the proceeds from poll taxes, but these trickled in much more slowly than expected, and meanwhile ships waited offshore, unable to dock because there was no cash to pay their crews. Seamen came in to be paid one by one, but often found themselves palmed off with tickets rather than money. When the Navy Office was short of money, as it frequently was, and they later attempted to redeem these tickets, they were repeatedly sent away and told to come back a week later. A black market quickly emerged; hard-headed dealers, mostly women, would give the sailors instant cash for their not instantly usable tickets – at a discount, of course.

On land and on their ships too, sailors suffered from diseases, the principal ones being scurvy and syphilis. The former is known to have affected

To Build a Lighthouse

Drake's crew on his round-the-world voyage in 1580, but it was not taken seriously until 1753, when *A Treatise on Scurvy*, the first systematic observation of a deficiency disease, was published, and citrus fruit recommended to boost vitamin C levels. Since one of the first symptoms of the disease is bad temper, it was implicated as a cause of mutiny – but a lack of vitamins was probably the least of the sailors' reasons for bad temper and revolt.

Into this maelstrom of misery for sailors swam Henry Winstanley, with a practical proposal conceived not by Trinity House, which supposedly had the best interests of sailors at heart, but by the private enterprise the Brethren so distrusted. Winstanley was infected by the virulent strain of entrepreneurialism which was taking hold of men with money everywhere. Men were taking more risks, no longer just following in their fathers' footsteps, but investing in weird and wonderful new schemes. A book on the investment fever of the late 1690s, published in 1720, lists among many others 'Companies for Mines . . . Diving of many sorts . . . Glass Bottles. . . Salt-Petre, Sword-Blades; Waters . . . Wrecks . . . Lifting-Engines, Drawing-Engines . . . Lotteries . . . New Settlements . . . Convex-Lights . . . Fisheries Royal and Private'. A lighthouse provided just one more investment opportunity – and a chance to make a mark on the world.

Many of the men who had these ideas, including Winstanley, were more showmen than hard-headed businessmen; many were irresponsible and ruined themselves and others. But at least Winstanley's enterprise, unlike most of the political plans and private lighthouse projects which preceded it, was closely linked to the plight of the ships such as his own which had been lost on the Eddystone, and was motivated by a desire for well-deserved fame rather than undeserved profit.

Winstanley rode into Plymouth at the very end of 1695, looking for information about how his ship the *Constant* had gone down. When he heard about the treacherous Eddystone reef he wanted to know why it was not marked with a lighthouse. The local fishermen explained that they were all in favour of having a lighthouse there, and even the king had said it should be built – but the question was, who was going to build it? Winstanley must have had a vision of the solution – a magnificent tower, higher than the highest waves, beaming out an unquenchable light into the darkness and warning sailors away from the perils of the rocks. The locals doubtless told him all about the treacherous currents, the slippery rocks, the difficulties of even approaching them – but he was Henry Winstanley, Gent. He had built a house of wonders and a fabulous waterworks. He could build anything. And if the king wanted a lighthouse, then what better way to advance his cause?

He would begin to build, he said, the following summer; by the next year his light would be operational. His plan was to erect a stone base, surmounted by an octagonal wooden tower containing living quarters, with a lantern at the top. The critics and the pessimists said it could not be done. They pointed out all the obstacles facing him – the problems of transporting men and materials, of fixing the stones to the wet and barnacle-encrusted rocks of Eddystone – and said the whole plan was preposterous.

> 'Give in, give in,' the old Mayor cried,
> 'Or thou wilt rue the day.'
> 'Yonder he goes,' the townsfolk sighed,
> 'But the rock will have its way.'

The task was certainly daunting. But Henry Winstanley, Gent., was undauntable. To ordinary people it might have looked impossible, but he was not ordinary (or rather, he was determined not to be). This was to be his finest hour. 'This gentleman had distinguished himself in a certain branch of mechanics, the tendency of which is to raise wonder and surprize', wrote John Smeaton; now this gentleman intended to provoke such reactions on a grander scale and with a different kind of mechanics than had previously been imagined.

Winstanley drew up plans for his building and submitted them to Trinity House; they were approved. The Brethren had in 1694 been granted royal leave to erect a lighthouse on the Eddystone and to charge a due of 'one penny per tunn outward bound and alsoe one penny per tunn inward excepting Coasters [i.e. vessels trading between ports along the same coast; these were to pay] twelve pence for each Voyage passing by the said Lighthouse or Beacon and noe more'. But they were appalled by the difficulty and expense of the undertaking, and only too glad now to hand over the reins to a private investor.

Up until the final signing of the agreement with Trinity House, Winstanley worked in cooperation with Walter Whitfield, who had first proposed a light for Eddystone four years earlier, but Whitfield disappeared as soon as they had jumped together this final administrative hurdle. Perhaps he died; perhaps he panicked at the thought of the expense, or at the sight of the big picture uncluttered by minor obstacles. Whichever was the case, in the early summer of 1696, the heady sound of the sea drowning out the sceptics, Winstanley set sail for Eddystone alone.

SEVEN

WINSTANLEY'S DREAM

For all his looks that are so stout,
And his speeches brave and fair,
He may wait on the wind, wait on the wave,
But he'll build no lighthouse there.

More is known about the building of the lighthouse than about any other aspect of Winstanley's life, partly because he wrote his own brief account of it, and engraved it in the sky on his picture of his lighthouse, and partly because the illustrious engineer John Smeaton, creator of the third Eddystone lighthouse in the 1750s, took the trouble to study what had gone before. He wrote a clear and generally sympathetic account some sixty years later, when Winstanley's work and his misfortune were still vivid in memory.

Winstanley's undertaking was guided neither by practical experience nor by reliable historical information. When Wren started building churches he may have wanted to do better than those who had gone before, but he at least had a whole country full of churches of one sort or another to admire and criticize and improve upon. But no one had ever built a lighthouse on a rock in the open sea; there was no precedent to be followed, nothing to tell Winstanley how high or what shape his tower should be if it were to survive the wind and the waves.

One major technical problem, and perhaps in the end the most significant shortcoming, lay in the cement. No one had yet discovered a composition that would set and stay bonded under water. Sixty years later Smeaton carried out a sequence of experiments in an attempt to find a waterproof formulation, but the problem was not completely cracked until sixty years after that, in the 1820s, by another Yorkshireman, Joseph Aspdin. In the 1690s, therefore, the basic mortars used to hold bricks and stones together were ill-suited to frequent immersion in sea water and to battering by the worst of the Atlantic weather. In Smeaton's opinion, this was the greatest weakness in the edifice of his predecessor. Nor did Winstanley make the most of the few historical examples that were available: various long-lasting lighthouses had been built using the same method of 'cementing' the stones together with molten lead as Sostratus had used at Alexandria two thousand years before.

Early in the summer of 1696 Henry Winstanley set sail for Eddystone. That is, metaphorically he set sail. Unfortunately the prevailing wind is from the south-west: it blew straight into his face. Beating to windward in a small sailing boat crammed with workmen and materials would have been slow, difficult and dangerous, and if they had been forced to resort to rowing – if the wind had blown up into a gale or faded to a flat calm – in a sailing boat cluttered with wet canvas, the difficulties would have been multiplied. So they had to go in a rowing boat.

When Winstanley reached the rocks and was able to reconnoitre at close quarters, he found that although the lethal reef covered a quarter of a square mile there was only a single rock big enough and high enough to form the foundation for a lighthouse. The others were most of the time covered by water, and their surfaces anyway too jagged to build upon. This one possible rock, known ever since as the House-Rock, has a surface about 10 feet above the water at high tide, and about 30 feet across; it is fairly flat, but slopes at about 30 degrees to the horizontal. In other words, it is like half a tennis court, tilted upwards so that one edge is level with the high wire netting.

On the lee side of this rock, to the north-east, there is deep water, and in calm weather it is possible, though not easy, to climb from a boat on to the rock, using natural handholds and footholds. At low tide a small level surface is exposed, almost a slimy landing stage, on to which materials can be landed. However, this rock is on the western edge of the Eddystone reef, exposed to the full fury of any weather from the Atlantic. Furthermore the approach to the lee side is through a narrow channel between the lines of jagged rocks – a challenge for even an experienced helmsman. A light wind is enough to whip up waves big enough to make landing hazardous; a mild Atlantic swell, causing the water surface to rise and fall by several feet every few seconds, makes it almost impossible to bring a boat alongside in safety. Smeaton summarizes the perils of the Eddystone rocks:

> when the sea is to all appearances smooth, and even, and its surface unruffled by the slightest breeze, . . . the sea breaks upon them in a most frightful manner, so as not only to obstruct any work being done upon the rock, but even the landing upon it, when, figuratively speaking, you might go to sea in a Walnut-shell.

The helmsman who slightly misjudges it may well find that when the boat falls with the swell it lands with a sickening scrunch on the vicious rocks below the surface. When lifted off by the next wave, the boat is like a sieve – and there are 14 miles of open sea between the rock and the mainland.

Only during the summer months was there any possibility of getting out and landing at the Eddystone. Every day that the weather allowed, Winstanley and his rowers would board their boat at the Barbican (the quayside in Plymouth) and leave on the high tide, helped by it out of the Sound. Heading due south, they hoped three hours later to catch the main ebb tide flowing westwards out of the Channel, which would speed them on their way. Six hours of rowing were needed to get to the Eddystone, but more often than not when they approached the reef they found the conditions there too rough for them to land. All they could do was turn round and row back again. Six hours each way, and nothing to show for their labours but aching limbs and blistered palms, which would have been more bearable had they been from tools and not just from oars.

Sometimes the weather turned against them, and they could not even indulge in the luxury of the six-hour row back to Plymouth, but had instead to seek shelter somewhere closer along the coast (at Rame Head, for example), forgoing their own beds for an unknown shore and the prospect of another long row when the weather cleared. Even when everything went to plan, it allowed at the most two or three hours' work at low tide, followed by the homeward journey and the prospect of the same sort of exhaustion the next day, and the next.

Winstanley's first objective had hardly seemed ambitious; he had had little to go on, but had formulated what seemed like a reasonable plan, in three easy stages. First, to gouge twelve small holes in the rock, and fix an iron in each by pouring in molten lead. Second, between and around the irons, and fastened to them by bands of iron, to build a solid stone base about 12 feet high, to bear the brunt of the sea's anger. Third, on top of the stone base, to build a wooden tower with living quarters and storage rooms, and surmounted by a lantern in which would burn the warning light. From the comfort of dry land this seemed pretty straightforward, but having once begun to suffer the violence and unpredictability of the weather, and the difficulties of transporting men and materials to Eddystone, Winstanley realized how grossly he had underestimated Nature, and the task ahead of him.

The problems began as soon as he heard about the *Constant*. He had to get down to Devon in the middle of winter. His journey from London to Plymouth must have taken almost a week on horseback; the roads narrowed and deteriorated as you travelled further west, until wagons could not pass and so riding was the only option. Indeed, other than in the city of Exeter, carriages and other wheeled vehicles were almost unknown in Devon until the eighteenth century.

More and more things needed to be moved around the country, but roads were not being built and improved proportionally. Turnpike tolls had been introduced in 1663, for much the same reasons as lighthouse dues, to pay for safer and more comfortable travel, but by the turn of the eighteenth century turnpike roads were still relatively rare. On her way through Devon heading for Land's End in 1698 Celia Fiennes wrote that beyond Exeter

> the roades contracts and the lanes are exceeding narrow and so cover'd up you can see little about, an army might be marching about undiscover'd by anybody . . . the wayes now became so difficult that one could scarcely pass by each other, even the single horses, and

so dirty in many places and just a track for one horses
feete, and the banks on either side so neer . . .

Devon's most valuable asset, its serges, had to be
taken to market loaded on long strings of pack
animals; Winstanley must have had to use the same
inglorious means to move his building materials.
Boats could be useful on this smaller national scale
of transport: the river network had been enlarged
and spruced up, and coastal trade also helped to
prevent the roads turning completely into swamps.
National trading was the little sister of the colonial
stuff, but not that much littler: fleets of colliers
made three thousand trips a year delivering coal
down the east coast to London – that was where
James Cook was to learn his seamanship sixty years
later – and the taxes raised from this trade went
towards paying for Wren's cathedral and his fifty-
two churches; seamen at Wapping referred to
Newcastle as the 'Black-Indies'. But whatever
means of transport Winstanley used to get himself
and his tools and stones and iron rods to the
quayside at Plymouth, it must have been pretty

slow and unreliable, owing to bad roads, bad ships and bad weather.

When he reached Plymouth, new difficulties emerged. He had hoped to complete the first part of his plan, the digging of the holes and the planting of the great irons, in a couple of weeks. But it was not to be so easy. First he had to choose his men, and no doubt that took some time. There were plenty of tough and willing seamen in Plymouth, but how many would remain enthusiastic when they heard about the job he planned for them? Then, because of the weather, he found that he could land on the rock perhaps only once a week during the summer, and even then for only a few hours at low tide.

This is what Winstanley himself had to say in the preamble to his *Narrative of the Building*:

The Light-house was begun to be Built in the Year 1696 and was more than four Years in Building; not for ye [the] Greatness of ye Work, but for ye Difficulty & Danger of getting backward and forward to the Place; nothing being or could be left safe there for ye first 2 Years, but what was most thoroughly affixed to the Rock . . . nothing could be attempted to be done, but in ye Summer Season; yet ye weather then at times would prove so bad yt [that] for 10, or 14 days together ye Sea would be so Raging about these Rocks, caused by out Winds and ye running of ye ground Seas, coming from ye main Ocean, that altho' ye weather should seem & be most calm in other places, yet here it [the sea] would mount and fly more than 200 foot, as has been so found since there was lodgment upon ye Place; and therefore all our Works were constantly buried at those times & exposed to ye Mercy of ye Seas . . .

When he did manage to get his men on to the rock their difficulties seemed to get even worse. Scrambling from a boat on to the slippery rock is difficult: Adam should know because he has done it — and he wasn't even carrying a pickaxe. Winstanley's first objective was to make twelve holes in the rock, but the red gneiss is incredibly hard, so hard that even a mighty blow from a pickaxe chips off only a tiny sliver of the rock. A strong man could hack away all day and scarcely be able to see any result from his work. Meanwhile the rock was slimy and covered with barnacles, and every now and then, even in the calmest weather, a wave would break over the top, wetting everything with salt spray. So the men were wet and cold, and the pickaxe handles slippery in their hands. A pick dropped off the rock sank without trace into the depths; a man who slipped off would probably be badly injured before he hit the water.

They started work on the rock in July, and had to stop less than two months later, when the days became too short and the weather too harsh to continue. In that summer of 1696 the only progress they managed was to dig twelve holes in the rock. The Victorian poet Jean Ingelow's effusive ballad captures the frustration:

> In fine and foul weather
> The rock his arts did flout,
> Through the long days and the short days,
> Till all that year ran out.

When the holes were deep enough Winstanley ferried out twelve great iron bars, each as thick as a man's arm and twice his height. On the rock, he had his men put a bar upright in each hole, and then, after lighting a fire and melting lead in iron pans, they poured molten lead around the great irons to fix them immovably into the rock. These irons would give them a solid anchorage from which to start the building – but not until the following summer.

Winstanley's own account is brief and to the point:

> The first Summer was spent in making twelve holes in ye Rock and fast'ning twelve great Irons to hold ye Work yt [that] was to be done afterwards, the Rock being so hard, & ye time so short to stay by reason of Tides or Weather, and ye distance from ye shore, and ye many Journeys lost yt there cou'd be no landing at all, and many times glad to land at our return at places, yt if weather permitted, would take up ye next day to get to Plymouth again.

Such sluggish progress invigorated the critics – who again said the task was impossible and the taskmaster a fool – but their disparagements in turn invigorated Henry Winstanley, Gent. Nothing was going to beat him, neither the onslaughts of the elements nor those of the sceptics; both were bracing to his courage and determination.

During the winter he returned to his wife and responsibilities in Littlebury and London, but by June 1697 he was back in Plymouth, hoping to complete his lighthouse during this second summer. He began by transporting huge stones out to the rock, and cementing them together within the circle of the Great Irons, to which they were bound by bands of iron. Gradually he built up a solid stone base for his tower. Once again the work must have been extraordinarily difficult. Every stone had to be cut to shape in Plymouth, ferried out to the reef, and then winched from the rocking boat, presumably using a block and tackle, on to the slippery, treacherous rock. In Winstanley's own words:

> The next Summer was spent in making a solid Body, or kind of round Pillar twelve foot high, and fourteen foot Diamiter, and then we had more time to Work at the Place, and a little better landing, having some small shelter from the Work and something to hold

by, but we had great trouble to carry off and to land so many Materials, and be forced to secure all things as aforesaid every night and time we left work, or return them again in the Boats.

On this occasion his progress was halted not by the weather but by the French.

Louis XIV's desire for French expansion and personal glory were illustrated not only in the ostentation and extravagance of Versailles – where 36,000 workers spent forty-seven years building and decorating the sumptuous gardens and apartments – but in thirty years of foreign wars. In 1697 these were beginning to grind to a halt, but there was still a residual rumbling conflict with England, and so the Royal Navy had been ordered, thanks mainly to Whitfield's earlier negotiations, to protect Winstanley and his men while they worked. The task fell to the *Terrible*, of which the captain's and lieutenant's logs still survive.

During this second summer the captain, Timothy Bridge, seems to have been helpful to Winstanley and sympathetic to the hardships of his men. For much of that summer he allowed them to sleep on board the *Terrible*, which meant that in the morning they merely had to be ferried across to the rock in a longboat, and no longer faced the six-hour row to and from Plymouth every day. This may not have improved the working conditions or the weather, but it did mean that they could climb on to the rock fresh and ready for work, rather than exhausted after six hours of rowing, and in calm weather it allowed them to work much longer hours on the rock.

This posting was something of a short straw for the crew of the *Terrible*. The routine quickly settled into uneventful tedium:

> at 3 in the morning we waighs and runs out to the Edystone, the long boat sets them on shore upon it, they works upon it all Day and at 8 at night the Boat fetched them on board. We laye by the Edystone all night as neare as we could keep, sometimes lying by and sometimes making a small trip to and again.

Unfortunately the sailors' diet was as monotonous as their duties, and, in the absence of more pressing concerns, as minutely documented:

we get up our Cables in order to take in Provisions and we
takes in 11 Baggs of Bread, . . . 1 Puncheon of Beef, . . .
1 Hogshead of Pork, . . . 1 Hogshead of Pease, 2 Firkins
of Butter containing 123 Pounds of Neat Butter . . .

The oppressive summer heat was unrelieved except
by happy accidents like that of 8 August: 'These 24
hours close Weather, this morning our Longboat
went out to the Edystone with the Engineers to
work. And at 10 this Morning found a boat with 12
Tunns of Beere, we took it in and stowed it and
coiled down our Cables and made all Cheare.'

The log does mention an incident when they
'sees the Privateere and gave him Chase all night
and then lost sight of him', but even such mini-
adventures were rare, and in the middle of the
summer the keen young commissioner St Loe
decided the ship was no longer needed for guard
duty, and allowed the captain to rejoin the main
fleet in the Channel.

Eager to win his spurs in the great British Navy,
Captain Bridge had hoped for a dangerous posting
where he could prove his heroism, and he felt
slighted by being sent on guard duty to protect a

dotty lighthouse-builder at Eddystone. He weathered the boredom of 'ply all day off and on the Stone' for a couple of weeks; once the building was high enough to be out of the waves most of the time the men would sleep on the rock, and he took the ship back dutifully each morning to guard them. But on 25 June the threads of patience and obedience, already frayed thin, were finally snapped by the irresistible sight of the rest of the fleet. The crew had been doing lots of gun-cleaning in hopeful preparation for action, and 'at ½ past 5 this morning Commissioner St. Loe came on board, we immediately weighed and stood off to ye grand fleet . . .'.

Unfortunately a snooping French privateer noticed the *Terrible*'s absence, and sailed up unmolested to the House-Rock, intent on destruction. The men at work on the rock had neither the time nor the means to defend themselves and their hard-won achievements. The rock was suddenly crawling with foreign sailors, armed to the teeth. The Frenchmen broke down the stones which had cost so much time and pain to transport and build up, and threw them into the sea. They stripped the Englishmen naked and set them loose in an open boat to shiver and pray for rescue; all but Winstanley, whom they chained up and ferried off to France, where he was thrown into gaol. All work on the lighthouse ceased; the critics crowed.

News of this outrage soon reached the Admiralty, which had been keeping a hopeful eye on the progress of the lighthouse. An Admiralty Minute dated 28 June reads: 'Resolved that Commissioner St. Loe be directed to give an account of how it happened that the workemen on the Eddystone were soe ill protected as that the Engineer was taken and carried to ffrance by a small ffrench challoope.'

The following day they sent a letter of displeased surprise to St Loe, demanding explanations, and on 3 July one of chilly protest to Louis XIV. Consulting his advisers, the Sun King was enlightened, and realized that capitulation would be a good tactical move; French sailors would benefit as much as English ones from a lighthouse in the Channel. Moreover Henry Winstanley was a well-known figure, and had been a friend of Charles II.

Louis commanded that the prisoner be released and brought before him. First he offered Winstanley 2,000 louis d'or to stay and work in Paris, perhaps tempted by the thought of having amusements and engravings to rival his counterpart's across the Channel and liven up the rather weighty elegance of Versailles, and no doubt in turn tempting Winstanley with the prospect of royal patronage. But the engineer's passion seems then to have been only for his lighthouse, and he politely declined. The king sent him back to England with a heap of presents and the sanctimonious declaration that the French were at war with the English, not with humanity.

Landing a few days later in Plymouth harbour, our hero did not take time to wallow in the good publicity which his adventure and its happy ending must have provided, but returned to his stonework, this time accompanied by a naval escort that did not wander off. However, several valuable

Louis XIV: Winstanley's Gaoler

Louis XIV was born in 1638. His father died when he was five and his mother ruled as regent on his behalf for eight years. When he was ten the Parisian revolts against high taxes became a personal threat, and he fled the capital, returning at the age of fourteen. He exercised rigid royal control, one of his ministers commenting that Louis 'sees everything, hears everything, makes every decision, gives every order'. He once said of himself, 'L'état c'est moi', summarizing even more neatly the absolute concentration of power in his hands. His liking for ostentation and extravagance is encapsulated in the spectacular Palace of Versailles. He supported the arts with enthusiasm, and encouraged playwrights such as Racine and Molière. He certainly merited his sobriquet the 'Sun King': the palace was a microcosm of French life, which revolved around the king like the planets around the Sun. He died in 1715, saying 'I depart, France remains', and the country did remain — with a tax system reorganized, to the benefit of the few, a vast palace, an army weary from wars and a flourishing art department.

weeks of summer had been lost. A more cautious routine was adopted, in which the *Terrible* sailed back to Plymouth every night with the workmen on board, often remaining weather-bound in harbour for days at a time, since that August was a stormy one. Once again the men had to transport, lift and position huge blocks of granite; there was always a compromise to be made between safety and progress, between trying to finish just one more block, and making sure everything was secure before casting off in good time. So there was no realistic chance of completion that year; in October work was brought to a standstill by autumn gales.

The tower, though, had visibly grown. They now had 'something to hold by'; the squat stone pedestal was almost ready for its statuesque wooden adornment. The stone base was a cylinder 14 feet across and 12 feet high; this, Winstanley reckoned, would withstand the full force of the waves, even in a storm – although since no one had ever been on Eddystone to see what a storm there could be like, no one could really imagine it.

Winstanley himself was to get a taste of the weather at Eddystone in the middle of the following summer, 1698, as he vividly describes:

> The third Year, the aforesaid Pillar or Work was made good at the Foundation from the Rock to sixteen foot Diamiter and all the Work was raised, which to ye Vane was eighty foot, being all finished, with the Lanthorn and all the Roomes that was then in it. We ventured to lodge there soon after Midsummer, for greater dispatch of this Work, but ye first Night ye weather came bad & so continued, that it was eleven days before any Boat could come near us again, & not being acquainted with the hight of the seas rising, we were most all ye time neer drowned with wet, & all our Provision in as bad a condition tho' we work'd night & day as much as possible to make Shelter for ourselves. In this Storm we lost some of our Materials altho' we did what we could to Save them.

This third phase of the construction was to build an octagonal wooden structure from the top of the stone, and Winstanley succumbed unreservedly to the extravagance of the fashion that was then dominating European design. In the seventeenth century European monarchs were more than usually concerned with proving and immortalizing their supremacy through magnificent and persuasive works of art. The highly theatrical baroque style, whose props were illusion and extravagance, gave rise with its transformation of natural shapes, alteration of classical proportions, and shrinking or expanding of space, to works that were suitably awe-inspiring. This style of surprise and elaboration entirely suited the showman in Winstanley, and he would have experienced its full splendours both in Paris, where it was given free rein at Versailles, and in the magnificence of Wren's St Paul's.

The basics of Winstanley's design were quite reasonable. His octagonal tower was altogether 80 feet high, from the rock to the very top. At the bottom came a store room, then a state room, an umbrella-shaped kitchen, and finally the lantern (or 'lanthorn' as he called it), an octagonal room with walls of glass so that his light would be visible in all directions. And since rumour has it that Winstanley may have been the man who, as a sideline, introduced top-quality Italian glass-making into England, smuggling craftsmen and their top-secret lead crystal-making methods out of Venice, it seems likely that he would have taken particular pride in this layer of his construction. The excesses began there.

Baroque immoderation suited him fine. There were gaudy paintings of blazing suns, rather reminiscent of Louis's self-glorifying emblem. On top of the tower was a huge weather-vane, supported by a colossal curly wrought-iron bracket. Although this must have cost a lot of time and money to make, transport and haul to the top, and although it must have acted as a sail in the wind, trying to topple the structure with every gust, Winstanley did not have the benefit of inborn restraint or modesty; he was a pioneer, and he was determined that his lighthouse would be noticed at all costs.

Few records remain of this first incarnation. Jaaziell Johnston painted the lighthouse, although it is not known whether he did so on site, as he claimed, or whether he worked at second-hand, from Winstanley's sketches for instance, rather than braving the swell and the spray which constantly enveloped the rock and its new occupant. Either way, an engraving of this painting made by I. Sturt captures the unprecedented wonder of the construction (see plate section). The other testimony was created for posterity by Winstanley himself; basking in success, he commissioned from the prominent Plymouth goldsmith Peter Rowe a silver salt – an elaborate salt-cellar – in the form of an exact model of the lighthouse.

Salt was an important and expensive commodity from the Middle Ages onwards, and so to own and display a silver salt was to show off your wealth and social position. The City of Exeter presented a salt in the shape of a castle for the coronation of Charles II, and the City of Portsmouth presented one to his wife, Catherine of Braganza. Winstanley's was most unusual both in being so ornate and in being for private use.

Winstanley's salt (see plate section) stands 19 inches high, weighs 17 ounces and comes apart in separate pieces; the cupola and the perforated lantern form a sugar caster; the gallery below contains a hollow for salt (although it is rather inaccessible); and the lower part of the structure divides into three compartments, of which the central one has a perforated lid and could have been used for pepper. Winstanley was delighted; he claimed to have paid more than £90 for it, and he installed it among the other curiosities in his House of Wonders. You can still see it today in Plymouth Museum, and it remains as beautiful and as impractical as was its short-lived inspiration.

The final stages of the building work in this third summer must have been much easier and more efficient, because the crew could camp out in the building, and therefore work all through the daylight hours, instead of having to spend time rowing to and from a ship, not to mention having to wait for the few precious hours at low tide. By this time Winstanley probably had two complete crews, one ferrying out supplies, the other in residence and working on site.

In Plymouth there was growing fascination and speculation about what life would be like with a light on the Eddystone. Fiennes, strolling around Plymouth's citadel, wrote:

> had a view of all the town and alsoe part off the main Ocean, . . . there you can just discover a light house which is building on a meer rock in the middle of the sea; this is 7 leagues off it will be of great advantage for the guide of the shipps that pass that way; from this you have a good reflection on the great care and provision the wise God makes for all persons and things in his Creation, that there should be in some places, where there is any difficulty, rocks even in the midst of the deep which can be made use of for a constant guide and mark for the passengers on their voyages; but the Earth is full of the goodness of the Lord and soe is this Great Sea . . .

Her concept of the Eddystone as a godsent marker of the eddies of the Sound, rather than as the cause of them, is rather curious, and her praise of God to the exclusion of Winstanley would probably have irritated him – but at least she, an ignorant Londoner, was showing due interest. Even as the work gathered momentum in its final stages, though, there were many who still said that it would never be finished, that the lights would not stay lit in a wind, that their feeble glow would be invisible from half a mile away.

So it must have been with pride, excitement and a supreme sense of achievement, not to mention a charitable satisfaction in the benefit it would be to humanity (combined no doubt with a little uncharitable pleasure at having defeated his detractors, at having forced the unbelievers to believe), that at nightfall on Tuesday 14 November 1698 Henry Winstanley climbed up into the almost-completed lantern and lit the sixty tallow candles one by one. It was a windy night; they flared, they guttered – but they kept burning, warning the sailors of the rocks below. It was the first time a lighthouse had ever shone from a rock in the open sea, and it was a triumph for Henry Winstanley, Gent.

In Plymouth there was pandemonium. The fishermen coming in from the sea reported that they had seen a light on Eddystone. For the first time ever they could see in the dark where the dreaded reef lurked. Their lives would never be the same again. Rapidly the rumour spread, hardly believed at first: Winstanley had really done it, Winstanley had lit the Eddystone. What had already in 1586 been referred to by Camden in his monumental *Britannia* as *scopulos infamis* – infamous rocks – in a phrase borrowed from Horace's description of a similar menace in the Mediterranean; what had been known for years as the 'dreaded' Eddystone, had finally been marked and tamed. Crowds scrambled up on to the Hoe and to Rame Head to see whether they could spy the new beacon with telescopes – it was just about possible, and though the homely candle flames were not stunningly bright their mere presence was stunning; there must have been much mirthful rejoicing in homes and pubs, and tearful celebration in the streets.

The only people who did not join the celebrations were the now celebrated Winstanley and his crew. They were stuck out on the rock, and the weather was so bad that it was five weeks before they could get back to land. By the time they returned, just before Christmas, their affection for the lighthouse must have been waning. They had almost run out of candles for the lantern and food for themselves, since no one had planned for such a long and early exile:

> we returned again, and finished all, and put in the light on the 14th of November 1698. Which being so late in the year, it was three days before Chrismas before we had a relief to get ashore again, & were almost at the last Extreamity for want of Provisions, but by Good Providence then two Boats came with Provisions, and ye Family that was to take care of the Light, and so ended this years Work.

EIGHT

A STATELY HOUSE ON THE SEA

*The winds blew, and beat upon that house; and it
fell not: for it was founded upon a rock.*

Winstanley may never have confessed to his
anxiety, but he must have been shaken by the storm
of which he had had such a long and unobstructed
view just before Christmas 1698; the tales that the
keepers told of their winter on the rock must also
have alarmed him. We do not know what the
'family' sent to relieve the workers just before
Christmas was composed of, nor what stretches of
time they spent there. But that long winter trapped
on a rock, whose loneliness even the most
devotional monk or hermit had never coveted,
would have pushed any married couple to the
limits of their own resources – and their love for
one another. There was no escape – from the
weather, or from each other's company.

The wooden walls of the lighthouse must often
have seemed very thin. The keepers must have told

Winstanley of the shuddering of the tower in the wind and waves; of how the lighthouse rocked so much that their crockery was shaken off the table, and they were thrown out of bed, and made seasick. He himself knew that the lantern was often drenched; and that waves broke right over the top of the tower as if it were no more than a sandcastle on the beach. The ragged state of the cement, only two winters old, was another physical warning. As soon as the weather was good enough to allow it, he started building again.

The fourth Year, finding in ye Winter ye effects the sea had on this house, and Burying the Lanthern at times, altho' more than sixty Foot high, early in the spring I encompassed ye aforesaid Building with a new Work of four foot thickness from ye foundation, making all solid near 20 foot high, and taking down the upper part of the first Building, and enlarging every part in its proportion, I raised it 40 foot higher than it was at first, and made it as now it appears, and yet the Sea in time of storms flies, in appearance, 100 feet above ye Vane & at times doth cover half the side of the House and the Lanthorn as if it were under Water.

He created virtually a whole new lighthouse. He increased the thickness of the stone base from 16 to 24 feet, and its height from 12 feet to 20. To counteract the imperfections of the cement and secure the mortar from the wash of the sea, he added girdles of iron or copper plate to every joint. The wooden structure was also added to, made taller, stronger, grander; an extra bedroom was squeezed in between the kitchen and the lantern room, in addition to the existing 'very fine Bedchamber, with a Chimney and Closet, . . . richly Gilded and Painted'; the octagonal column was made twelve-sided; the old ladder was replaced by an internal staircase; a gallery now encircled the lantern, and it was said that through the open gallery, with a high tide and a high wave, a six-oared boat could be carried.

As well as these structural improvements, Winstanley made more idiosyncratic additions. He set up a swing with a seat to lift visitors in comfort from boat to front door, as well as a crane to lift provisions; and a chute designed for casting down stones on enemy invaders, perhaps hoping for an opportunity for revenge against the likes of the privateers who had once found him defenceless.

Naturally, he made a strikingly elaborate engraving of the lighthouse once it was finished (see plate section). This reveals much both about the lighthouse itself and about Winstanley and his priorities. Suspended in the sky in the top left-hand corner is a humble dedication to His Royal Highness ye Prince Lord High Admiral of England, encased in a frame of mythological gods, sea creatures, globes and seaweed. This takes up almost as much space as the adjacent text, which is Winstanley's account of the entire construction of the lighthouse. Suspended below it, floating in the breeze, is a red ensign as tall as the lantern room itself; both further proof, were it needed, of his lasting esteem for status and resulting fervent nationalism.

Elsewhere, pleading succour of the Almighty, though perhaps also bordering on blasphemy, he emblazons each of the eight sides of the lighthouse, just below the open gallery, with a pious, or simply grandiose, maxim. *Post Tenebris Lux* ('After Darkness, Light'); *In Salutem Omnium* ('For the Safety of All'); *Pax in Bello* ('Peace in War', perhaps referring to the constancy of the rock in the midst of seething seas – or simply to the provision of safety despite the war with France); and 'Glory be to God', read those visible on the engraving. Above them all, however, is another dedication to King William – closer to heaven than his 'God'.

The tableau gives a powerful sense of the flamboyance of the structure, loaded with accoutrements and dwarfing the sailing ships behind it and the minuscule figures who peer from its windows, hoist flags and throw ropes from the rock. Quite apart from its size, no tediously cylindrical tower would do for Winstanley the showman; likened by some to a Chinese pagoda, this octagon above has become a dodecagon below, the whole festooned with decorations, a stately home with state rooms and balconies:

Henry Winstanley

A strange sight I have seen:
. . . a stately house one instant showed,
Through a rift, on the vessel's lee:
What manner of creatures may be those
That build upon the sea?

He must have known about the famous elaborately decorated tower at Cordouan, and although his had to be smaller he was probably determined that it would be just as perfectly formed — for it to be a wedding cake just as artistically iced as that of de Foix. And, crowning the front door, he manages to squeeze in the best inscription of all:

Hanc PHARON

Designavit et

struxit

H. WINSTANLY

de LITTLEBURY

In Com. ESSEX

Gent. Anno Dom

1699.

Or, in English, 'H. Winstanley Gent. of the county of Essex designed and built this lighthouse, AD 1699.'

Hanc PHARON
Designavit et
struxit
H. WINSTANLY
de LITTLEBURY
In Com. ESSEX
Gent. AnnoDom
1699.

The inscription above the door of Winstanley's lighthouse.

The Latin original makes sense, except that there is no word 'Gent' in Latin, but Winstanley wanted everyone to recognize his stature as a cultivated entertainer, architect and pioneer – so he put it in anyway. The whole point of the lighthouse was to keep ships away from the reef, which meant that no one would ever come close enough to read this inscription – but that clearly did not worry H. Winstanl(e)y, Gent. (Curiously Winstanley with an e appears in the dedication at the top left, but Winstanly without an e in three other places on this engraving.)

The engraving provides full information on the workings of the lighthouse in the complex key on its right-hand side:

A. The Rock on ye landing side, with ye strong iron Rail leading to ye entring Door, where is shown ye Bolts and Eyes to ffasten ye door, and round iron steps for entrance.
B. An Engine Crane yt parts at joynts to be taken off when not in use, the rest being fastened to ye side of ye house to save it in time of storms, and it is to be made use of to help landing on ye Rock, which without is very difficult.

C. The Window of a very fine Bedchamber, with a Chimney and Closet, the Room being richly Gilded & Painted, & ye outside shutters very strongly Barr'd.

D. A Gallery to take in Goods and Provision from ye Boat to the store Room.

E. The State Room, being 10 square, 19 foot wide, & 12 foot high, very well Carved & painted, with a Chimney, & 2 Closets, & 2 Sash Winden, & with strong shutters to Bar and Bolt.

F. The Airy or open Gallery where is Conveniency to Crane up Goods & a great Leaden Cestern to hold ye rain Water that falls from ye upper Roofes in leaden Pipes; and to let ye Sea pass through in time of storms.

G. The Kitchin where is a large Chimney, Oven, Dressers & Table, with a large Closet, and a large standing Bed etc.

H. A Bedchamber with 2 Cabbin Beds, & all Conveniencies for a Dining Room with large Lockers to hold a great store of Candles for lights.

I. The Lanthorn yt holds ye light is 8 square, 11 foot Diameter, & 15 foot high in ye upright Wall: having 8 great Glass windows and ground Plates for Squares, & conveniency to burn 60 candles at a time, bisides a great hanging Lamp. There is a door to go into ye Gallery, that is all round to cleanse ye Glass of ye

Lanthorn which is often dim'd by salt water yt
washeth it in storms.

K. is great woodden Candlesticks for Ornament, but
ye irons yt bears them is very useful to stay a ladder to
clean ye Glass.

And so on. Item K is a lovely example of
Winstanley's somewhat defensive justification of
his extravagance, and he does not even mention the
huge and unjustifiable weather-vane on top.
Perhaps the real lighthouse was never really like
this. Perhaps this liberal encrustation with its
flagpoles and finials, ornamental candlesticks and
inaccessible compasses existed only in Winstanley's
mind and in his engraving. Yet, while the picture is
well seasoned with artistic licence – there is a
veritable armada of tall ships sailing past,
improbably close to the rocks, and there should be
other rocks visible, even at calm high tide – close
inspection shows us the practicalities of
Winstanley's construction. He knew how difficult
it was to land on the rocks, and he had to provide
other means of getting provisions on to the
lighthouse. Cranes on both the east and west sides

of the building must have given boatmen a reasonable chance of landing supplies of food, water and candles, even in moderately bad weather and with a moderately good helmsman, on whichever side was then in the lee of the rocks.

Nature was not entirely against him; the House-Rock is part of a ridge that runs roughly north–south. In the prevailing westerly wind and swell, this acts as a sort of breakwater, creating a calmer patch of water to the east, where there is a narrow channel between the other rocks. This is therefore the best place to approach by boat, although skilful piloting is needed to avoid several other rocks within twenty yards or so – to the extent in fact that Eddystone became an unofficial testing ground for boatmen. A particularly competent one, James Bound, was press-ganged by the Navy as a result of his rock-landing prowess, and Winstanley had to make a formal complaint through a Trinity House agent in order to secure the return of the man 'upon whom was all his dependence in landing at the house where nobody else could or would venture'.

No one was going to visit Winstanley's lighthouse for pleasure or curiosity – 28 miles in an open boat was hardly a jolly Sunday outing – but its fame spread much further than its salutary beam. With his usual hard-headedness, Winstanley linked advertising of the lighthouse and Littlebury; the engravings promoted the house and the house was a place to buy prints of the engravings. Along the bottom of the 1699 engraving runs the mantra: 'This Draught was made & Engraven by Henry Winstanly of Littlebury Gent. and is sold at his Waterworks: where also is to be seen at any time ye Modle of ye said Building & principal Roomes for six pence a Peice.' In the garden at Littlebury, to entice visitors, he built from brick a second model of the lighthouse a few feet high. This in turn must have helped to promote his Waterworks in London. It was a wondrous and irresistible trio of Winstanleyana.

In Plymouth, Winstanley had long been a hero, an uncontested one since the candles had first been lit. 'Mr Stanley', wrote one correspondent from the town on 29 November 1700, 'has much obliged the ships yt come this way by building a fine lighthouse on the Eddystone & so making . . . safety which before had been fatal to many.' Trinity House naturally tried to steal the limelight. Three days after the candles were first lit, it ordered the following notice to be inserted in the *London Gazette* and to be posted at ports around the country, with the aim of encouraging captains to pay ungrudgingly the dues for the light's support:

> The Masters, wardens, and assistants of Trinity House having at the request of navigation, with great difficulty, hazard, and expense erected a light-house upon a dangerous rock called the Eddiston, lying at the mouth of Plimouth Sound, as well for the avoiding the said rock as for the better directing of ships thro' the channell and in and out of the harbour aforesaid. They doe hereby give notice that the said light hath been kindled for some time; and that being discernible in the night at the distance of some leagues, it gives entire satisfaction to all masters of ships that have come within sight thereof.

Winstanley must have been furious at their temerity. Who was it, after all, that had braved all the difficulty, hazard and expense of building a lighthouse, without a scrap of practical support from the men who were supposed to be responsible for lighting the coast? But there was really no need to resent this slight for long. Winstanley was now a national celebrity: people knew his name, whether or not it featured in government announcements. Less illustriously perhaps, but with a broader audience, he was sung about in the music halls. One song is the lament of a merman whose mermaid mother made the mistake of falling for the lighthouse-keeper; his two siblings are exploited by humans – an ironic lament on the way the poor perils of the sea, such as the sirens, had been tamed by the building of the light:

My father was the keeper of the Eddystone Light
And he slept with a mermaid one fine night.
From this union there came three –
A porpoise and a porky and the other was me!

Yo ho ho! The wind blows free;
Oh for a life on the rolling sea!

A Stately House on the Sea

One night while I was a-trimming of the glim,
And singing a verse from the evening hymn,
A voice from the starboard shouted 'Ahoy!'
And there was my mother, a-sitting on a buoy.
Chorus

'Oh where are the rest of my children three?'
My mother then she asked of me.
'One was exhibited as a talking fish,
And the other was served in a chafing dish.
Chorus

Then the phosphorus flashed in her seaweed hair,
I looked again and my mother wasn't there.
But her voice came echoing out through the night
'To hell with the keeper of the Eddystone Light!'
Chorus

More important to Winstanley, his work was again recognized by the king. Following the death of Charles II in 1685, and the three uncomfortable years of James II's Catholic fanaticism, William of Orange, James's nephew and son-in-law, and James's daughter Mary had on 13 February 1689 been jointly proclaimed king and queen. While still a prince, William had stayed overnight at Audley End on at least one occasion, and Winstanley may have been presented to him then, but there would have been no reason for William as king to pay much attention to Winstanley while he remained no more than an ambitious engineer. Now, however, Winstanley had supplied the lighthouse that William himself had demanded a few years earlier, and the king had every reason to be impressed and appreciative. Indeed, proof of his interest in Winstanley's enterprise comes in the fact that he commissioned Thomas Bastin, an artist who made his money sketching important buildings, to make pictures of the lighthouse for him, both before and after its improvement; by 1702 the paintings – probably the artist's most exalted commission ever – were hanging in William's rooms at Kensington.

Winstanley was now no longer a young unknown. Henry Winstanley Gent. had arrived. No one in the world could hold a candle to his ingenuity, his skill, his extraordinary courage and tenacity. Sailors of all nationalities were grateful;

Winstanley's Dedicatee:
William III His Royal Highness ye Prince Lord High Admiral of England

William of Orange first met Mary, James II's eldest daughter, when she was only eight; they were married when she was fifteen in the strict privacy of her bedchamber late at night. She managed to alleviate the miseries of living in Holland with a short and asthmatic husband by taking up garden design and starting a collection of blue and white china. It was only her existence that kept the English indulgent of their king's Catholicism.

When a son was born to James's queen (see p. 8), robbing Mary of her place in the succession, her husband rushed to England to safeguard the throne; in 1689 they were jointly crowned as sovereigns. After his victory at the Battle of the Boyne in 1690, William was a hero to Irish Protestants, who referred to him affectionately as 'King Billy', but he was never so popular with his English subjects; he was too cold and serious for their taste, and too short on personality.

no ship was wrecked on Eddystone while Winstanley's light stood there. Yet his critics, in particular the die-hard Puritans of Nonconformist Plymouth, remained distinctly unimpressed by Winstanley's metropolitan flamboyance, and still sniped away. They heard about the storms and the remedial work that Winstanley had done, and they found a new chink in his armour. Every year they chorused that it would never survive another winter; every winter they were proved wrong. Every time a gale blew, they made light of it and said that a real storm would destroy the lighthouse.

In the end Winstanley lost patience with their tedious prophecies of doom and retorted in kind. On Thursday 25 November 1703, during a brief respite from bad weather, he decided to return to the Eddystone to effect some urgent repairs before winter set in. The story goes, according to Smeaton, that as he stepped into the boat on the Barbican the fishermen warned him that the storm was not over, and that 'dirty' weather was going to whip up again; they advised him not to go out. He ignored them. He was fed up with being told what he could and could not do. He, Henry Winstanley Gent., knew about the sea and the weather at Eddystone, and he said that his crowning wish was to be in his lighthouse for the greatest storm that ever blew under God's heaven.

He set sail, and his wish was cruelly granted.

NINE

THE GREAT STORM

Stay we within? Dangers hang o're our Head,
Our *Houses* are our *Refuge* and our *Dread.*
But step we forth? *The boist'rous* Tempest *brings*
A thousand Deaths *upon her rapid* Wings.

Henry Winstanley had boasted that his crowning
wish was to be in his lighthouse during the greatest
storm there ever was. The gales had been blowing for
days, and the vicious waves, not to mention the
cutting wind, must have made it an uncomfortable
voyage out to the exposed rock – and how exposed it
must have felt that November day. No doubt as he
entered the lighthouse, shutting it fast against the
weather, he became aware of how isolated Eddystone
was, of the fragility of the wooden structure he had
built, of the strength of waves and wind.

Wednesday 24 November had begun with calm,
fine, watery sunshine, after many consecutive days
of wild and savage winds – the young journalist
Daniel Defoe called it 'a calm fine day as at that

time of year shall be seen'. It was the calm before the storm – 'The Greatest, the Longest in Duration, the Widest in Extent, of all the Tempests and Storms that History gives any Account of since the beginning of Time', which would leave many a town 'the very Picture of Desolation, . . . as if an Enemy had Sackt it'. By the time Winstanley reached Eddystone, sailors would have been battening down hatches and retreating to safe harbours, in expectation of the fury that they could feel coming.

The Great Storm was an active remnant of an American hurricane, which had swept its way across the Atlantic, driving ships irresistibly before it into already overcrowded English ports. For two weeks there had been severe gales from the west, each day breaking records as the worst in living memory – chimney stacks were blown down in London, hundreds of tiles were blown off houses, several ships were lost. All the ships coming from the west were blown in ahead of schedule by the gales, and ran for shelter to the Channel ports. Those ships that were about to leave could have made no headway against the westerly gales, so they remained at anchor. And, reported Defoe, 'those ships which were newly gone to sea were forc'd back . . . so that the sea was as it were swept clean of all shipping'.

In contrast to this strangely pristine ocean was every port, every harbour, every estuary – all crammed with ships. Ships moored on moorings, to jetties, to one another, even just anchored in the open water. 'In Yarmouth there rode at least 400 sail. At Portsmouth and Cowes . . . almost 300 sail.' On Wednesday 24 November the wind died down, but then rose again and

> On Friday morning it continued to blow exceeding hard . . . towards Night it encreased: and about 10 a Clock, our Barometers informed us that the Night would be very tempestuous; the Mercury sunk lower than ever I had observ'd it on any Occasion whatsoever, which made me suppose that the Tube had been handled and disturb'd by the Children.

Defoe should have been less suspicious of his children and more trusting of the barometer; both were telling the truth. The Revd William Derham of Upminster recorded his barometer reading 28.72 inches between 12.30 a.m. and 6 a.m. on the fateful Friday morning, while the barometer at Towneley Hall near Burnley read 28.47 at 9.30 p.m. on Thursday and 28.50 at 7 a.m. on Friday.

By chance Friday was the night of the new moon; so it was completely dark, which meant that during the night no one could see what was happening outside. In the small hours of Saturday morning people lay sleepless all over Britain, afraid both to lie still and to move. Seized by fear in the darkness, people imagined they heard thunder when it was only the howling of the wind, and claimed, probably fancifully, to have experienced earthquakes: 'the Shaking and Terror of [their Houses] might deceive their Imagination, and impose upon their Judgment'. The atmosphere was apocalyptic:

the wind by its unusual violence made such a noise in the Air as had a resemblance to thunder . . . the Fury of the Wind was greater than was ever known . . .

> Together with the Violence of the Wind, the Darkness
> of the Night added to the Terror of it; and as it was just
> New Moon, the Spring Tides being then up at about
> Four a Clock, made the Vessels, which were a float in
> the River [Thames], drive further up the shore.

A new moon means a spring tide, and the westerly
gales turned this into one of the highest tides ever
known. When people later compared notes, this
super-high tide turned out to be a common feature
of coastal areas countrywide: 'In some parts of
England the tide rose six or eight Foot higher than
it was ever known to do in the memory of Man.'
These invading seas left many animals in the water
where they did not belong, and many boats on the
land where *they* did not belong. In Cardiff several
hundred sheep and some cattle were drowned, and
'one of the Market Boats was lifted upon the Key
. . . . In Burnham was driven five trading vessels as
Colliers and Corndealers . . . at least 100 yards on
Pasture Ground.' At Huntspill, near Wells, five
small vessels 'drove on shoar which remain there,
and 'tis supposed cannot be got off'. In
Southampton 'most of the ships in the river . . .

were blown on shore'. Fifteen thousand sheep were drowned in one Level on the bank of the Severn.

The winds were strongest in the hours before dawn, but by seven o'clock had begun to abate. One by one people peeped out of doors, 'the Distraction and Fury of the Night' visible in their faces as they were greeted by a desolation of fallen trees, and of houses and churches felled as easily. Ships crammed into harbours in futile defence against the storms had blown on to one another, on to rocks, on to the land; their havens had become hazards.

Daniel Defoe compared the storm of 1703 both to ancient biblical tempests and to more recent disasters, such as the Great Fire of London, finding the Storm more widespread and more severely destructive than anything previously experienced. Defoe, best known today as the author of *Robinson Crusoe*, was then only a young journalist but he had already honed his descriptive skills in his accounts of the Great Plague and the Great Fire. He was staying in London and recorded the 'miserable

Sight, in the Morning after the Storm, to see the Streets covered with Tyle-sherds, and heaps of Rubbish, from the Tops of the Houses, lying almost at every Door'. He saw tiles blown 30 or 40 yards from their rightful places, buried 5 to 8 inches deep in solid earth by the force of their fall, or, in the city, blown across streets and through the windows opposite. He toured Kent on horseback to assess the damage there, and placed an advertisement in the *Gazette*, asking for eyewitness accounts from around the country of the Great Storm of 26 November 1703. As a result we have a wealth of striking and probably fairly accurate – if sometimes dramatized – details of what happened that night. This was published the following year under the title *The Storm: or, a collection of the most remarkable casualties and disasters which happen'd in the late dreadful tempest, both by sea and land.*

In the countryside people were mesmerized by the sight of the 'Hay [that] was driven up into the Air, and flew about like Feathers'. Oats and barley became similarly airborne, but were less suited to long-haul flights because of their greater weight, and landed more quickly. From south-east England Mrs Dentram wrote of what she learned from the vicar of Lewes:

> a Physician travelling soon after the Storm to Tisehyrst, about 20 Miles from Lewes, and as far from the Sea, as he rode he pluckt some tops of Hedges, and chawing [sic] them found them Salt. Some Ladies of Lewes hearing this, tasted some Grapes that were still on the Vines, and they also had the same relish. The Grass on the Downs in his Parish was so Salt, that the Sheep in the morning would not feed till hunger compelled them, and afterwards drank like Fishes, as the Shepherds report.

The wind had been coming from the south-west, and Defoe notes with surprise and scientific curiosity that more tiles were blown off the lee side of houses than from the sides facing the wind. 'In many places . . . where a building stood ranging North and South', he writes, ' . . . the East-side of the Roof would be stript and untiled by the Violence of the Wind, and the West-side, which lay open to the Wind, be sound and untouched.' Small buildings in the lee of larger ones were often more damaged than those standing alone, not protected but endangered by their robust neighbours. At Christ Church Hospital, 'the building on the west and south side of the Cloyster was at least 25 foot higher than the East side, and yet the Roof on the lower side on the East was quite untiled by the Storm'. He put this down to eddies in the wind, but it was probably the result of turbulence on the lee side of the building causing lowered air pressure, which lifts the tiles off; scientists now call this the Bernouilli effect.

Such was the demand that the price of plain tiles rose in the course of a week from 21s (just over £1) per thousand to £6. This had the result that many houses remained roofless all winter, while others were festooned with more imaginative coverings made of wood – of which there was no shortage of naturally hewn pieces – or anything else that was going cheap.

Tiles had been blown off roofs before, but this time heavy lead roofing, like that of Westminster

Abbey and Christ Church Hospital, 'was in many places roll'd up like a roll of parchment, and blown in some places clear off the Building'. During the Great Fire lead roofs, including that of the earlier St Paul's Cathedral, had melted and run down both inside and out, ruining crypts and graveyards; what happened to the lead now was even more spectacular. At Leamington Hasting in Warwickshire not only did the lead on the church roof roll up like a Swiss roll, but six sheets of the stuff, weighing at least 2.5 tons, were carried 50 yards through the air before a tree blocked their way.

The brand new 100-foot church spire at Stow was blown down, and fell through the church roof 28 feet away. Ben Bullivant from Northampton reported that the lead on the three church roofs there rolled up like scrolls, and a huge elm tree was blown in a great arc from a park into a road without even grazing the wall in between. In St James's Park alone a hundred elms came to grief. At Ilminster two huge beeches, with trunks 5 feet thick, were broken like straws; likewise an oak tree at Besselsleigh near Oxford. John Evelyn, a man of horticultural obsessions and author of *Sylva, or a Discourse on Forest Trees*, mourned 'the subversion of woods and timber, both ornamental and valuable, through my whole estate, and about my house the woods crowning the garden-mount, and growing along the park-meadow . . . is almost tragical, not to be paralleled with anything happening in our age . . .'.

Defoe himself, riding around Kent on horseback, had begun to count the uprooted trees, but 'left off reckoning after I had gone on to 17,000; and . . . I have great reason to believe I did not observe half of the Quantity'. Through Oxfordshire a column of wind and water – today it would be called a tornado – marched with the gale, leaving a trail of flattened grass, trees and houses. An oak tree in its path snapped, weak as a sapling; the spout passed over a road, sucking the puddles dry; it passed over a cottage, sucking up the thatch; then passed into the distance. Throughout the country more than four hundred windmills were overturned and broken to pieces 'or the sails so blown round that the Timbers and Wheels have heat and set the rest on fire, and so

The Great Storm

burned them down'. The extent of the destruction can be judged from Defoe's advice to his readers: 'Those towns who only had their houses untiled, their barns and hovels levelled with the ground, and the like, will find very little notice taken of them in this account.'

The death toll was limited by the fact that the worst of the storm occurred during the early hours of the morning, when most sensible people were indoors and in bed, but even so 123 people were recorded as having been killed by flying tiles and falling stacks and walls. A woman and child who made the mistake of being outside in Brecon in the small hours were blown away by the wind – how and where they landed is not revealed. Even beds were no guarantee of safety. More than eight hundred homes were blown down, beds and all; in others, bedrooms became the targets for deadly pieces of 'top-hamper' falling from the roofs. Mr Simpson, a scribe living in Threadneedle Street in London, was woken by his family and warned of the danger of the storm, but 'too fatally sleepy, and consequently unconcerned', he turned over and went back to sleep. Minutes later the chimney-stack fell and killed him where he lay. He was not alone in paying for his laziness; two thousand chimneys blew down in London; twenty-one people were killed by them and more than two hundred were 'very much wounded and maim'd', many in their own beds.

Woken from his slumbers by the wind, as it overpowered the weakness of his decaying castle, the Lord Bishop of Bath and Wells foresaw the collapse of the ceiling of his bedchamber, leaped from his bed and made for the door. Here 'he was found with his Brains dash'd out; his Lady, perceiving it, wrapt all the Bed-cloaths about her, and in that manner was found smothered in Bed'.

Some were luckier. The number of tragedies is almost matched by the number of 'remarkable Deliverances'. The minister of South-Ash was just getting out of his bed when a chimney landed upon it; he was unhurt except for a few squashed toes. The Registrar of Eton College, staying at the Bell-Savage Inn in London, was carried by the momentum of a falling chimney-stack from his first-floor bedroom down to ground level; happily his bed fell with him. Pregnant women went into premature labour induced by 'the Fright of the Storm', and in many cases gave birth without the assistance of midwives, who could or would not fulfil their professional or charitable duty.

Far from proving human fortitude in the face of adversity, the storm in many places shows only the strength of human selfishness. At Poplar, 'a Gang of hardened Rogues' broke into a house in the most tempestuous hours of the storm; they matched its violence with their own, attacking the family and stealing their possessions. All the townspeople of Deal, a port just north of Dover, were accused by Defoe of particularly 'great Barbarity in neglecting to save the Lives of abundance of poor Wretches'. These wretches were the sailors whose ships had succumbed to the waves and had broken up. To the pieces of wreckage, the remnants of masts and rigging, the sailors clung, and many half-swam, half-drifted on to the Goodwin Sands, at low tide a stretch of sea-darkened sand cut off from the mainland. The men made ever more desperate signals for help, fearing the rising tide which would return them to the mercies of the rollers and the undertow, helpless as flotsam. Using telescopes like opera-glasses, the townspeople impassively watched the actors on their distant stage. Finally a boat set out for the Sands – the sailors thought themselves saved – but the boat flew like a vulture over the waves towards the carcasses of the ships, took its fill of the pickings and returned to shore more slowly, gorged and unwieldy.

Only one man was moved to humane action by the sight of the suffering. Thomas Powell, the town mayor, 'a Man of Charity and Courage', hurried to the Custom House to ask for men and boats to act as rescuers. He was rudely refused. So he turned instead to his fellow citizens, not so naive as to appeal to their altruism, but rather going for their business acumen. He offered to pay them five shillings for every life saved. Several agreed grudgingly to go, if he provided the boats. Forced to become plunderers themselves, risking position and reputation, the mayor and his men took the Custom House boat, then those which had just been engaged in piracy. In the few hours left before the creeping tide covered the sands, two hundred men were saved, but 'all that were left were swallow'd up with the Raging of the Sea'. Later, with houses full of refugees, the mayor applied for aid to the Queen's Agent for Sick and Wounded Seamen – but the cunning agent found an escape clause, an excuse not to give a penny to those who clearly were sick and wounded seamen. At his own expense, therefore, the mayor provided the survivors with meat, drink and lodgings, and later transport to London; at his own expense he buried those who did not survive. Eventually he obtained a small and grudging reimbursement from the government; he at least did not go bankrupt as a result of his humanity.

The Storm brought tragedy to some, salvation to others; sometimes a mixture of the two. One boat, tossed for hours by giant and merciless waves, was just on the point of splitting up altogether – the timbers cracking, the water creeping, then rushing in through the rents in the timbers that seemed as flimsy as cotton. The sailors – two men and a boy –

braced themselves to plunge into the icy waters. Suddenly another boat appeared on the crest of a wave. Its rowers fought to keep some control, and drew close enough for one of the men to jump to safety, then the other. The boy jumped last, but his feet slipped, and he slid into the sea and was lost.

At Whitstable, on the Medway, a boat was lifted up by the violence of the wind like one made of paper. It rolled over and over in its airborne voyage, and in its erratic, mesmerizing course it struck human flimsiness, leaving a man crumpled, his knee shattered, in its turbulent wake. Only the solidity of a grassy slope checked its progress; in this the boat embedded itself, its own anchor.

The most dire destruction, however, was of the ships crammed like sardines into every available inshore space. The Navy lost twelve ships and 1,611 men, and the losses in merchant shipping were worse: in harbours and estuaries eight thousand sailors drowned that night within yards of the shore. John Crabb, a Fellow of Exeter College, Oxford, wrote in a poem inspired by the storm:

The Great Storm

Ships are but *Cock-boats*; *Cables* are but *Threads*;
Main-masts but *Straws*, and spreading *Sails* but *Shreds*;
Anchors Cobwebs; *Folly* the *Pilot's Skill*;
When *Heaven* has decreed we shall speed *ill*.

'The ship call'd the Shrewsberry that we are in,' reported one correspondent to Defoe from the Downs, 'broke two anchors, and did run mighty fierce backwards, within 60 or 80 Yards of the Sands, and as God Almighty would have it, we flung our sheet Anchor down, which is the biggest, and so stopt. Here we all pray'd to God to forgive us our Sins, and to save us, or else to receive us into his Heavenly Kingdom . . . I have not had my Cloaths off, nor a wink of sleep these four Nights, and have got my Death with cold almost.'

Such despair and self-pity are magnified in the account of a foundering ship limping in from the West Indies on the tail of the gale. Where the masts used to be were nothing but splintered stumps; what used to be a sleek and majestic hull was now more a collection of holes and cracks. The captain and surgeon abandoned their men to their fate, and took their lives into their own hands: 'by a fatal Contract, as soon made as hastily executed, they resolv'd to prevent the Death they feared by one more certain; and going into the Cabbin, they both shot themselves with their Pistols'. Their cowardice had made them too hasty; the captain lived just long enough to tell the tale, just long enough to hear those on deck cry out that the ship had been driven by the wind and tide safely into harbour. Then he too died of loss of blood from his bullet wound.

As for the Eddystone, the Great Storm must have been even worse there than it was on land. We can imagine Henry Winstanley listening to the howling and screaming of the wind and wondering . . .

> The great mad waves were rolling graves,
> And each flung up its dead;
> The seething flow was white below,
> And black the sky o'erhead.

So was he screaming triumphant abuse at the wind and waves? Was he with icy calm methodically monitoring the structure of the building? Was he terrified and praying? We shall never know. Shortly before midnight on Friday 26 November Eddystone was seen to be showing its light as usual. By the time the sun came up on Saturday morning, there was no sign that the lighthouse had ever existed, apart from a few twisted pieces of iron sprouting from the rock. No wreckage was ever found, nor any trace of Henry Winstanley, Gent.

EPILOGUE

Two days later, on Sunday 28 November 1703, the crew of the brig *Winchelsea*, coming in from the Atlantic richly laden and battered by the storm, could see neither the familiar beam of light nor the lighthouse. The ship struck the Eddystone Reef and was lost with all hands. She was the first vessel to founder on the Eddystone for five years.

Daniel Defoe reported one aspect of the Storm, which was invested with the weight of superstition: 'It was very remarkable, that, as we are informed, at the same time the light-house above-said was blown down, the model of it in Mr Winstanley's house at Littlebury in Essex, above 200 miles from the light-house fell down, and was broken to pieces.'

Smeaton later sceptically remarked that it was hardly surprising 'that the same general wind that blew down the lighthouse near Plymouth might also blow down the model of it at Littlebury', but the locals believed in the significance of the shattered model, which was apparently the only object, the one ornament in the whole of the cluttered house, to fall to the ground. When it fell in the early hours, the neighbours said, Jane Winstanley knew she had become a widow.

In most respects, though, she lacked this kind of sentimentality; rather, she displayed in looking after Winstanley's interests an astute pragmatism which would have made her husband proud. A new edition of the popular engraving of the lighthouse was issued after his death; an inscription on the leaves of an open book tells of his tragic end and concludes with lucrative melodrama: 'This Fatall Peice which was his last Work, may serve for his Monument the House being his Tomb the sea his Grave.'

She continued to run the House of Wonders and the Waterworks, and also persistently angled for a pension from the queen, claiming that very little of her husband's investment had been reimbursed and that 'his widow being left in very mean circumstances was a fit object for her Majesty's charity'. She was finally granted £100 a year, on the condition that she remain unmarried, and therefore presumably needy; when she did marry again – to a French actor – she managed to keep it secret and to carry on reaping the harvest sown by her first husband's ingenuity.

Meanwhile the storm whipped up religious fervour across the country: '*The Lord hath his way in the Whirlwind, and in the Storm, and the Clouds are the dust of his Feet.*' For Defoe and his contemporaries, the horror and devastation of the storm of 1703 was to be compared with the wind sent by God to bring about the Deluge; to the ancient storm He sent to punish sinners – '*God shall rain upon the Wicked, Plagues, Fire, and a horrible Tempest*'; and to the lightning which set ablaze the cities of Sodom and Gomorrah. Here was incontestable proof of God's existence, and a warning of the punishment that would be meted out to the non-believer: 'I cannot doubt but the Atheist's harden'd Soul trembl'd a little as well as his House, and he felt some Nature asking him some little Questions; as these – *Am I not mistaken? Certainly there is some such*

Epilogue

thing as a God —What can all this be? What is the Matter in the World?' Defoe, like many of his time, was incapable of seeing rain as just rain and hearing nothing in the sound of the wind but moving air; and he assumed that even the most blindly irreligious would see God in the wind and the rain as clearly as he did.

The winds of 1703, as far as Defoe was concerned, lay beyond the boundaries of the scientific investigation that might be capable of penetrating more mundane natural phenomena. In the wind might be felt the weight of God's hand, both punishment and warning to his people: 'more expressive and adapted to his Immediate Power . . . more frequently made use of as the Executioner of his Judgments in the World'. Many were scared back into the fold, if only temporarily, by the disaster, their piety induced by fear. *'Preces & Lachrimae*, Prayers and Tears, the Primitive Christians Weapons, we had great plenty of to defend us withal,' wrote one Vicar. 'O that we were so wise as to consider it, and to *sin no more lest a worse thing come upon us!* That it may have this happy Effect upon all the sinful Inhabitants of this Land is, and shall be, the Dayly Prayer of Dear Sir, . . . *Your real Friend and Servant* . . .' wrote John Gipps.

By 2 December the winds had dropped to a flat calm, and a whole month of merciful dryness followed, letting people repair the damage in less discomfort; but consciousness of moral imperfection and the heavy hand of heavenly punishment probably tortured the minds of Gipps and his parishioners for much longer. Nearly two months after the Great Storm, on 19 January 1704, churches filled to overflowing throughout Britain for a commemorative public fast held to give survivors a chance to remember and to repent. No one wanted to admit that these disasters were largely random, that the cause of the storm was meteorological, for such an admission would acknowledge the futility of human existence: without the possibility of sin, renunciation and reform they would be bereft of hope; hope of the avoidance of further disasters.

Epilogue

Despite, or perhaps because of, the Great Storm – notwithstanding the loss of the building with which he had hoped to be remembered by posterity – obituaries recognized Winstanley as a Great Man. Defoe wrote that he was 'a Person whose loss is very much regretted by such as knew him, as a very useful man to his country. The loss of that light-house is also a considerable Damage, as 'tis very doubtful whether it will ever be attempted again, and as it was a great security to the Sailors, many a good Ship having been lost there in former times.' Another contemporary describes his death as:

> very considerable to this Kingdom, he being the most extraordinary Person in this Nation, for Inventions of that Nature, might have lived to have done great Good; besides, he was upon several Projects of great Consequence; one of which was the Fishery, in which he proposed to employ 20,000 men.

We have no idea what this Fishery might have been, but Winstanley's great ingenuity and talents were clearly, at last, respected; he really had become a man of Consequence.

Winstanley's was the first in a series of lighthouses built on the Eddystone. The same rock subsequently formed the foundation first for Rudyerd's lighthouse, begun exactly ten years after Winstanley and his men had first rowed out to the rock; later it bore Smeaton's light. John Smeaton completed his lighthouse in 1759, and it stood for 130 years, until not it but the rock itself was felt to be unsafe. The top half of the tower was removed to Plymouth Hoe, where it remains as a tourist attraction. The bottom half, known as Smeaton's Stump, was left on the rock, and there it still stands, in incredibly good condition after 240 years of the buffeting of wind and water. The pointing between the stones looks almost new, and the only damage is to the unprotected top of the sawn-off tower (see plate section).

Today Eddystone is marked by the Douglass Lighthouse, completed in 1888. This is run automatically, without permanent keepers, and sports a helipad on top for ease of access, if not aesthetic appeal. This modern construction looms high over Smeaton's Stump; it stands on another rock, about 20 yards away, which is only completely clear of the water at low tide, and was therefore not practicable for the simpler technologies of Smeaton, Rudyerd and Winstanley.

NOTES

xvi 'He erected the first . . .' Advertisement, 1709, in 'Exhibitions of
Mechanical and other Works of Ingenuity', BL 1269 h.38, f. 105.

1 'The troubled *Ocean* . . . John Crabb, *A poem on the late storm and
hurricane, with an hymn*, London, 1704.

5 'To avoid this terrible rock . . .' Samuel Smiles, *Lives of the
Engineers*, 1862.

7 'Plymouth is 2 Parishes . . . Christopher Morris (ed.), *The
Illustrated Journeys of Celia Fiennes, 1685–c.1712*, Webb & Bower and
Macdonald & Co. (Gulliver) 1982, pp. 201–3.

11 'Then stepped two mariners . . . Jean Ingelow

11 'I will take horse, . . .' Jean Ingelow

12 'It would appear to those . . .' Smeaton, Bk 1, Ch. II, p. 13.

14 'Too large for a King, . . .' James I.

16 'Infinite the crowd of people . . .' Samuel Pepys, 1660, p. 35.

16 'So glorious was the show . . .' Samuel Pepys, 1661, p. 79.

16 'The talk of the town . . .' Samuel Pepys, 1661, p. 71.

22 'From Cambridge . . .' John Evelyn, *Diary* (ed. de Beer), p. 353.

29 'Every artist . . .'   Havelock Ellis, *The New Spirit*.

43 'The undertaker of this great work . . .' The engraving of Winstanley's
House at Littlebury, Essex, is now in the British Museum.

49 'The fam'd house . . .' *Post Boy*, 18 December 1712.

49 'I saw those ingenious Water-works . . .' John Evelyn, *Diary*, 20
June 1696.

59 'It is immediately behind St James Park . . .' Quoted in R. Altick,
The Shows of London.

Notes

60 'The vessell is thus made . . .' Henry van Etten, *Mathematical Recreations*, 1633, pp. 128–9.

61 'Water work . . .' John Ashton, *Social Life of Queen Anne*, 1883, p. 219.

72 'I saw her mainsail . . .' Jean Ingelow.

93 'To give light . . .' St Luke 1:79.

118 'Give in, give in . . .' Jean Ingelow.

120 'For all his looks . . .' Jean Ingelow.

151 'The winds blew . . .' St Matthew 7:25.

156 'A strange sight . . .' 'Winstanley: an Apology', *Songs with preludes*, pp. 586–7.

170 'Stay we within? . . .' John Crabb.

BIBLIOGRAPHY

For further information about the Eddystone and other lighthouses, you might like to look at these books:

Beaver, Patrick, *A History of Lighthouses*, Citadel Press, 1973

Hague, Douglas B. and Christie, Rosemary, *Lighthouses: their architecture, history and archaeology*, Gomer Press, 1975

Majdalany, Fred, *The Red Rocks of Eddystone*, Longman Green & Co. Ltd, 1959

Semmens, Jason, *Eddystone – 300 years*, Alexander Associates, 1998

The texts we consulted during our research include the following:

Addison, William, *Audley End*, Dent, 1953

Altick, Richard D., *The shows of London*, Cambridge, Mass: The Belknap Press of Harvard University Press, 1978

An exact relation of the late dreadful tempest . . ., London, 1704

An historical narrative of the great and tremendous storm . . ., London, 1769

Beaver, Patrick, *A History of Lighthouses*, Citadel Press, 1973

Berry, John, *Playing Cards of the World*, Guildhall, London, 1995

Bird, Thomas, *Notes & Queries*, 8th series, II, 10 December 1892

Bowle, John, *John Evelyn and his world – a biography*, Routledge & Kegan Paul, 1981

Chapman, John, and André, Peter, *A map of the County of Essex*, 1772–4

Crabb, John, *A poem upon the late storm and hurricane, with an hymn*, London, 1704

Bibliography

de Beer, E.S. (ed.), *The diary of John Evelyn*, Oxford University Press, 1926

Defoe, Daniel, *The storm; or, a collection of the most remarkable casualties and disasters which happen'd in the late dreadful tempest*, London, 1704

Dictionary of National Biography, Oxford University Press

Evelyn, John, *The Diary of John Evelyn*, vol. 5: 1690–1706, Oxford, Clarendon Press 1955

Ewald, William Bragg, *The Newsmen of Queen Anne*, Oxford, Blackwell, 1956

Fournier, Felix A., *Playing Cards, General History*, Heraclio Fournier SA Vitoria, 1982

Hague, Douglas B. and Christie, Rosemary, *Lighthouses: their architecture, history and archaeology*, Gomer Press, 1975

Hart-Davis, Adam, *Chain reactions*, National Portrait Gallery Publications, 2000

Heffer, R. and Manyard, G., 'The Winstanleys', *Essex Review*, vol. xxix, p. 65.

Holmes, Geoffrey, *The making of a great power: late Stuart and early Georgian Britain 1660–1722*, Longman, 1993

Hoppit, Julian, *A land of liberty? England 1689–1727*, Oxford University Press, 2000

Larn, Richard, *Devon Shipwrecks*, David & Charles, 1974

Larn, Richard, and Larn, Bridget, *Shipwreck Index of the British Isles*, vol. 1, Lloyds, 1995

Lewer, H.W., 'Henry Winstanley, Engraver', *Essex Review*, no. 108, vol. xxvii (October 1918), p. 161

Lyle, R.C., *Royal Newmarket*, Putnam & Co. Ltd, 1945

Majdalany, Fred, *The Red Rocks of Eddystone*, Longmans Green & Co. Ltd, 1959

McCormick, W.H. *The modern book of lighthouses*, A. & C. Black Ltd, 1936

Bibliography

Morris, Christopher (ed.), *The illustrated journeys of Celia Fiennes 1672–c.1712*, Webb & Bower and McDonald & Co. (Gulliver), 1982

Notes & Queries 12th series, X, 29 April 1922, p. 331

Pepys, Samuel, *Everybody's Pepys: the diary of Samuel Pepys 1660–1669*, G. Bell & Sons, 1926

Picard, Liza, *Restoration London*, Weidenfeld & Nicolson (Orion), 1997

Quarrell, W.H. and Mare, Margaret (trans. & ed.), *London in 1710 from the travels of Zacharias Conrad von Uffenbach*, Faber, London, 1934

Semmens, Jason, *Eddystone – 300 years*, Alexander Associates, 1998

Smeaton, John, *Narrative of the building and a description of the construction of the Edystone lighthouse with stone*, 2nd edn (corrected), 1793

Smiles, Samuel, *Lives of the engineers*, 1862

von Uffenbach, Zacharias Conrad, *Merkwürdige Reisen Durch Niedersachsen Holland und Engelland*, Frankfurt & Leipzig, 1753, pp. 482–3

Wayland, Virginia, *The Winstanley geographical cards*, Wayland, Pasadena, California, 1976

Wheatley, Henry B., *Round about Piccadilly and Pall Mall, or a ramble from the Haymarket to Hyde Park*, Smith & Elder, London, 1870

Williamson, David, *The kings and queens of England*, National Portrait Gallery Publications, 1998

INDEX

Note: **Bold type** refers to main entry; *italic type* refers to entries in boxes

Index

Index

Index